17^{50}

HOW TO ENJOY OPERA

HOW TO
Enjoy Opera

by James Camner

DOUBLEDAY & COMPANY, INC.
GARDEN CITY, NEW YORK
1981

Library of Congress Cataloging in Publication Data
Camner, James.

How to enjoy opera.

Discography: p. 169
Includes index.
1. Opera.   I. Title.
ML700.C18   782.1
ISBN: 0-385-15850-5
Library of Congress Catalog Card Number 80–2325

This book is dedicated to the three divas in my life: my Aunt Leonora who turned on the radio to a Met broadcast for my first opera exposure, my mother who had to "support the habit" for many years, and my wife Connie without whose help this book would have been impossible.

ACKNOWLEDGMENTS

I am grateful to all the friends who have helped me with this book and wish to thank Stanley Appelbaum, Jordan Massee, Richard Arsenty, Bismarck Reine, Jean Jackman, Betty Ann Stewart and Carol Mann for their help and encouragement; the opera companies and tourist authorities for the many illustrations; and my editor at Doubleday & Company, Inc., Louise Gault. Most especially I wish to thank my wife, Connie, for her work and contributions to this book, which make her virtually a co-author.

James Camner

CONTENTS

Introduction   xi

Chapter One: WHAT IS AN OPERA?   1

Chapter Two: YOUR FIRST OPERA   13

Chapter Three: WATCHING AN OPERA   21

   La Bohème   22
   Faust   28
   Aida   34
   Tannhäuser   39
   Don Giovanni   43
   Orfeo ed Euridice   51

Chapter Four: FRONT ROW CENTER   61

   The Singer   61
   The Conductor   72
   The Stage Director   75
   The Designer   76
   Ballet in Opera   78
   The Audience   82

Chapter Five: WHERE TO SEE AN OPERA   87

   Opera in the United States (The Major Companies)   87
   Regional Opera in America   95
   American Opera Festivals   100
   There to Write for Tickets and Information:
        U.S. Opera Houses and Festivals   104
   Opera in Europe and Abroad   107

European Opera Festivals   115
Where to Write for Tickets and Information:
    European Opera Houses and Festivals   120

Chapter Six: OPERA'S BURIED TREASURES   123

Chapter Seven: OPERA ON TELEVISION
    AND IN MOVIES   129

Chapter Eight: OPERA ODDITIES   133

Chapter Nine: OPERA MYTHS
    AND MISCONCEPTIONS   143

Chapter Ten: THREE MISUNDERSTOOD TERMS
    AND PHRASES   153

    The Golden Age of Opera   153
    Bel Canto   155
    Coloratura   157

Appendix I: READING ABOUT OPERA   159

    Publications   160
    A Basic Reference Library   163

Appendix II: OPERA ON RECORD   169

    A Basic Opera Library on Record   170
    Related Works   177
    A Library of Historic Performances   179

Appendix III: CHRONOLOGY OF
    IMPORTANT EVENTS   185

Appendix IV: THE LANGUAGE OF OPERA,
    A GLOSSARY   194

Index   198

INTRODUCTION

What a wonderful, crazy and delightful experience opera can be. Triumphal marches, tender, lyrical singing, thundering ensembles and soul-stirring climaxes combine to make it unique and the most colorful entertainment in the theater.

Of course the founders of opera had none of this in mind. In about the year 1580, a group of Florentine music scholars determined to revive the ancient Greek theater, which had combined the elements of music, dance and drama. What has evolved from those *favole in musica* (stories in music), the phenomenon we know as opera, has all of these things, but it is doubtful that *Aida* bears any resemblance to Greek tragedy. We cannot say whether the ancient Greeks would be puzzled by a modern opera performance, but most twentieth-century audiences certainly are.

Why does a woman who is about to be assaulted stop to sing a tender plaint? Why do the onstage lovers sing to the audience instead of to each other? Why does an English-speaking audience sit quietly during a performance given in a foreign language and at the conclusion shout its approval in Italian? How can one introduce oneself to opera without becoming discouraged or turned off?

In this book we will try to answer this last question and others in order to make it possible for the novice to attend and enjoy a performance with some sense and knowledge of what is actually happening on stage. It is important to know which operas to go to first and which to avoid first, what records to buy and books to read and how to make sense of some of the more peculiar conventions of opera. There is a special section in

Chapter 2 concentrating on how properly to introduce opera to children, a task which should be no harder than introducing it to adults but is often neglected from an erroneous idea that opera is too heavy or too sophisticated.

People who think that they do not like opera will be surprised at how receptive they can be to it. For some, it will only be a slight change from classical symphonic music. Others who do not like classical music at all will find that they have already enjoyed a form of opera through musical theater: there are few people who have not enjoyed the music of *Oklahoma!* or *West Side Story*. The aim of this book is to introduce the most familiar body of works which are often classified indiscriminately as grand opera. Many of these works are products of the eighteenth and nineteenth centuries and are the main topic of discussion in this book as they form the backbone of the repertory of the world's opera houses. But the reader will see that opera is a living art form which is ever changing.

As this book is directed toward those who are interested in opera as a source of pleasure and entertainment, we have tried to concentrate on these aspects, while avoiding dry, scholarly dissertations as much as possible. Thus, we've kept dates to a minimum; but for those so inclined, we have listed the proper reference books in a later section.

CHAPTER ONE

What is an opera?

Opera is for everybody. It appeals on many different levels and in several ways; it appeals to lovers of music and of singing and to the casual listener interested in the richest and most exotic entertainment in the world. There is a special excitement in attending an opera. A hush falls over the audience as the conductor takes his place. Then the overture begins and you find yourself in another world. Perhaps in a Parisian garret at the turn of the century or in an ancient Egyptian palace. Not only is there drama, there is comedy, sometimes broad, sometimes very subtle. Audiences over the world have laughed with pleasure when Falstaff waddles or Don Pasquale minces across the stage. In Mozart's *Marriage of Figaro* the audience is treated to comedy and suspense considered shocking and revolutionary in its day, but which now inspires warm amusement.

As originally conceived by musicians in Renaissance Florence, opera was to be a rebirth of ancient Greek drama. It was known at that time that the great plays of the ancient world were performed to music, particularly the part of the chorus. On this line the Florentines, among whom were the composers Jacopo Peri and Giulio Caccini, laid the groundwork for opera. They envisioned it a unison of all the arts: music, drama, dance and painting, each playing an equal part. Despite all of the changes and evolutions opera has undergone through the centuries, the greatest lyric masterpieces have always followed these guidelines.

The first operas were relatively simple affairs with the drama emphasized through uncomplicated music. The words were declaimed rather than sung and these early *favole* (stories) permanently established the importance of understanding the words. Within fifty years, however, the singers had effected a dominance over opera which has lasted to the present day despite the efforts of composers, conductors, stage directors and managers to subdue them. Their solos, known as arias, were increasingly emphasized with each singer in a particular work being allotted a number of arias and duets according to the star status each enjoyed. This allotment more than the story determined the numbers of solos and duets. The aria began as the pause or reflective comment on an event or action in the opera, a sort of singing soliloquy which quickly became more elaborate as a vocal display piece for the singer.

Early singers were trained in composition themselves and regarded the music as a skeleton, to be fleshed out by their own ornaments and embellishment, and composers wrote the music to accommodate this practice. At this point, opera had become a very stylized affair in other ways as well. It was almost invariably based on Greek mythology or ancient history and was known as opera seria. Spectacle had become as important as the singing, and the scenery was lavish on a scale that has never since been approached. "Old master" quality painting on flats, or canvas backdrops, gave the illusion of vast temples and gardens, the painters of which became world-famous, especially the Bibbiena family. Costumes were also very lavish and the singers would add plumage and jewels to complete the splendor. In France the development of opera was similar, but was dominated by dancers rather than singers. In fact, one of the first "stars" of French opera was the Sun King himself,

PLATE 1. *Baroque opera and ballet are presented with authentic sets and costumes at Sweden's Drottningholm Court Theater near Stockholm. (Photo courtesy Swedish National Tourist Office)*

Louis XIV, in dancing roles. Such was the importance of the dance in French opera that until comparatively recently no opera could be staged at the Paris Opéra without a ballet.

In Germany, Italian opera seria was the accepted form. In fact, opera seria reached its peak with the works of a German composer who wrote in an Italian style, George Frideric Handel, whose *Julius Caesar* was considered by no less an authority than George Bernard Shaw to be the very greatest opera ever written.

Opera seria was codified in the libretti of Pietro Metastasio, whose classic opera seria libretti were set to music over and over again. Such was his influence that his name was usually printed more prominently on announcements and playbills than that of the composer.

But opera seria presents many problems to the modern producer. Without spectacular scenery these operas can appear very static. Even more difficult is the casting problem, as opere serie were composed for an extinct breed of singers known as the castrati (see the Glossary, Appendix IV), whose voices were said to have combined the ethereal purity of a choirboy's voice with the power of a mature adult's lungs and art, and from contemporary accounts the effect seems to have been sublime. Their vocal feats, if we are to judge by the music written for them and contemporary criticism of them, were unrivaled, and the music, if it is to be performed today, has to be simplified. Since the castrati were still men although their voices were in the female ranges, today the roles must be played by women or transposed downward for men, neither of which solution is ideal. Still, opere serie contain some of the most exalted music written by such composers, in addition to Handel, as Henry Purcell, Georg Philipp Telemann, Antonio Vivaldi, Claudio Monteverdi and Wolfgang Amadeus Mozart, and it is well worth the trouble to stage them.

By the time Mozart was writing opere serie, the castrati were already falling out of favor, and he wrote his most important opera seria, *Idomeneo*, for a tenor, although the second lead was written for a castrato. When Mozart later staged the work, he eliminated the castrato part altogether. By that time, the end of the eighteenth century, women were beginning to assume their now dominant role in opera as the prime donne, or leading ladies. The tenor was increasingly cast as the "lover boy" and the poor bassi were with few exceptions cast in the fatherly roles familiar to today's audiences. Actually, when the prime donne supplanted the castrati it was simply one type of soprano replacing another as the lead, indicating that audiences have always preferred this voice range to all others. Since soprani were originally the castrati, this is why the Italian word survives today in the masculine gender.

While Italian opera seria was at its height, little one-act comic operas known as intermezzi were often presented during intermission. Actually there were no intermissions as we know them today. The whole auditorium was kept lit throughout the entire evening's entertainment and the audience came and went, freely conversing and eating. Despite the distractions, these relatively simple affairs, which used usually two or three or even only one singer and which were really only to allow the opera seria performers to rest between acts, became so popular that they were expanded into the longer comic operas which are known as opere buffe. Opera buffa allowed the librettist and composer more freedom, since all types of stories were used, many with contemporary settings. Everything about opera buffa was less rigid and this no doubt partly explains why the oldest opera in today's popular repertory is a buffa opera, *La Serva Padrona* by Giovanni Pergolesi. Because opere buffe were rarely cast with castrati and since they used less stylized stories, they are very accessible to today's audience. They are best-known through the great Mozart and Gioacchino Rossini comic operas which brought opera buffa to its greatest artistic heights. *Don Pasquale* by Gaetano Donizetti is the last great buffa opera of the nineteenth century, although the twentieth-century composer Ermanno Wolf-Ferrari was a true master of the genre and his too infrequently performed *Il Segreto di Susanna* and *Il Campiello* are comic masterpieces.

In Germany the comic opera was known as the Singspiel (song-play) and followed a similar development to that of opera buffa. These often had fairy-tale or supernatural stories and reached their zenith with a Mozart opera, *Die Zauberflöte*, or *The Magic Flute*. Singspiel combined spoken dialogue with the music, as opposed to the recitative of opera seria and buffa; recitative is a declamation to music played by the orchestra, called *recitativo accompagnato*, or on the keyboard, called *recitativo secco*.

Some composers were becoming tired of the Baroque excesses of the opera seria form even while these works were enjoying their greatest popularity, and the great Christoph Willibald Gluck began the resistance to opera seria with his "reform" opera *Orfeo ed Euridice*, with its libretto by Ranieri Calzabigi and streamlined story and score, free of many of the excesses Gluck felt were inherent in opera seria. These reforms and the growing popularity of opera buffa, with its free use of modern stories, helped lead to the demise of opera seria in the eighteenth century.

With the dying out of opera seria and the castrati, dramatic opera evolved into a less formal style of opera: grand opera. Many elements were retained from the earlier forms, including sets almost as lavish, but the stories were often adapted from current popular romances and the recitative disappeared as the arias and duets blended more into continuous singing and ensemble.

By the time of Donizetti and Giacomo Meyerbeer, the early nineteenth century, grand opera was fully established. Ensembles, popular in buffa works but little used in opere serie, became prominent in grand opera. Famous examples include the sextet from Donizetti's *Lucia di Lammermoor* and the quartet from Verdi's *Rigoletto*. Still, the aria remained the backbone of the musical and dramatic structure. Grand opera of the nineteenth century includes these perennial favorites: Donizetti's *Lucia di Lammermoor*, *Rigoletto*, *Aida* and *Otello* by Giuseppe Verdi, Meyerbeer's *Les Huguenots* and *Le Prophète*, and the early Wagner operas *Tannhäuser* and *Lohengrin*. All of these lend themselves to grandiose and lavish staging. Most opera houses pull out all the stops when they present them.

Parallel to the development of grand opera was that of comic opera, which evolved from opera buffa and Singspiel format into comic light opera and operetta.

Operetta as an art form is usually considered distinct from opera, that is grand opera, but it really bears only slight differences and often follows the forms of grand opera in order to satirize it. The dramas are often farcical and seldom realistic; the music may be less demanding on the singers but, at its best, is still on a very complex and sophisticated level. Operetta reached a very high plane in the Viennese, French and English schools. Historically, each of these schools was dominated by one great composer or team. In France Jacques Offenbach, with the librettists Henri Meilhac and Ludovic Halévy, wrote works which made him famous as the "Mozart of the Champs-Élysées." In Vienna the great Strauss family dominated the light opera stage, especially Johann Strauss (II), whose *Die Fledermaus* is often performed in the world's major opera houses. In England the comic operas of William S. Gilbert and Arthur Sullivan are a national institution.

Although everyone is certain that opera and operetta are very different, people are less sure when asked to define the differences. What makes an operetta different from grand opera? Primarily, there remain long stretches of spoken dialogue in an operetta. Dancing is less formal and reflects more of a burlesque (nineteenth-century fashion—not striptease!) tradition. In some works, however, like *Die Fledermaus, The Yeomen of the Guard* by Gilbert and Sullivan, and Offenbach's *La Belle Hélène*, the differences become even less clear, and, in fact, these works are often done by grand opera companies. Actually, one of the most famous of all operas, usually presented as a "grand" opera, was written with spoken dialogue and can therefore be considered an operetta. This is the beloved *Carmen* of Georges Bizet, which some have called "the perfect opera."

It is certainly a mistake for anyone to regard operetta as somehow inferior to its more austere relation; certainly there is no more disciplined art form than the works of Gilbert and Sullivan. Descended from the ballad operas, such as *The Beggar's Opera* (1728) by John Gay, which satirized the florid opere serie of Handel, G&S operas combine time-honored burlesque traditions and contemporary satire into something unique. Their loyal following is even stronger today than when they were first performed a century ago.

At the end of the nineteenth century grand opera went through two further stages of development. In Germany under the activity of Richard Wagner it became a "music drama" with the dominance of the aria finally broken. The heavily orchestrated music is continuous and traditional set pieces or arias are almost nonexistent. This movement was really very brief; apart from Wagner, only Engelbert Humperdinck and Richard Strauss gained much prominence.

Italian grand opera's last trend at this same period was the development of verismo, or realistic, opera, as represented by the enormously popular works of Giacomo Puccini and those of his contemporaries, Pietro Mascagni, Umberto Giordano,

Ermanno Wolf-Ferrari and Alfredo Catalani. These composers
were attempting to break away from the romanticism of the
nineteenth century by the use of realistic, sometimes brutal
stories of passion and sex (not so very different from
nineteenth-century grand opera at that!). The style of the music
was streamlined, featuring lush, rich scores and soaring arias
with a premium on the size of a singer's voice and a minimum
of ornamentation and subtlety. This has remained the style of
singing to this day and has become an international style of
sorts, with the unfortunate result that nineteenth-century
grand operas and sometimes even eighteenth-century operas are
sung in this style as well. The most popular verismo operas include *La Bohème, Tosca* and *Madama Butterfly* by Puccini,
Cavalleria Rusticana by Mascagni, *Pagliacci* by Ruggiero Leoncavallo and *Andrea Chénier* by Giordano.

In France, however, the nineteenth-century grand opera style
continued to dominate, with Charles Gounod and Jules Massenet carrying on in traditional form. These composers were of
course influenced by Wagner and the early verists but managed to remain essentially French. This French school of the
late nineteenth century was characterized by refinement and
Gallic elegance, but without the cultivated techniques of this
French style of singing, it may sound banal today. Of lasting
popularity are *Faust* and *Roméo et Juliette* by Gounod.

The final European phase of opera is usually referred to as
"modern opera." Although most are now sixty and seventy
years old, they are still called "modern," which shows the resistance they have met in being accepted into the popular
repertory. Some of the well-known modern operas are *Pelléas et
Mélisande* by Claude Debussy, Alban Berg's *Wozzeck* and
Lulu, and *Peter Grimes* by Benjamin Britten. While these operas are celebrated and familiar names, they have all failed in
what Verdi among others considered the ultimate criterion: the
box office. They are just not universally popular and, considering the time the public has had to get used to them, it is doubtful that they ever will be. Of the above it is the operas by Alban
Berg and his mentor Arnold Schoenberg, who attempted to
change music totally from the tonal to the atonal, that are

hardest to take. They employ what is known as *Sprechgesang*, or speech-song. This hysterical screaming has ruined many a good voice. Modern composers appear to fear melody, perhaps thinking that it is pandering to the public's bad taste. Fortunately, while the intellectual modernists were composing in their ivory towers, there were others at work and it is to them that we look for the most recent development in opera: musical theater, especially as represented by the American, or Broadway, musical.

The Broadway musical evolved from the Viennese comic operetta and British comic opera and is the true opera of today, although a "serious" opera will be presented with much fanfare, such as *Antony and Cleopatra* by Samuel Barber which opened the new Metropolitan Opera House at Lincoln Center, or the recent *Paradise Lost* by Krzysztof Penderecki in Chicago. For while the "serious" new operas disappear with shocking regularity, the Broadway musical seems to be enjoying a permanency and resilience similar to that of grand opera of the past. Many classic Broadway musicals form a standard repertory and are constantly being staged. These include *Show Boat*, by Jerome Kern, and *Oklahoma!*, *South Pacific*, *The King and I* and *The Sound of Music* by Richard Rodgers and Oscar Hammerstein II. All of these works have much in common with their operatic ancestors, fulfill the guidelines set by the Renaissance Florentines and are all far more popular than the contemporary "serious operas." For instance, Benjamin Britten's most famous opera, *Peter Grimes*, was written in the same year as *Oklahoma!* Few can recall the melodies and arias from *Peter Grimes* while almost all are familiar with the music of *Oklahoma!*, a work which is constantly revived with success. Many critics now feel that *Show Boat* and *Carousel* are more truly "operatic" than "Broadway" in any case, while *Porgy and Bess* has even been staged at the hallowed La Scala in Milan. The recent Broadway hit *Sweeney Todd* by Stephen Sondheim is an extraordinary work which has been widely praised by music critics, many of whom have written that it is the great opera of our time. *Sweeney Todd* combines comedy and tragedy in a manner which is actually reminiscent of Mozart's

PLATE 2. *The Houston Grand Opera production of the classic American opera* Porgy and Bess. (*Photo courtesy Houston Grand Opera*)

PLATE 3. *Angela Lansbury and Len Cariou in the Broadway hit* Sweeney Todd, *a work more opera than musical.* (*Photo courtesy Martha Swope*)

Don Giovanni and might also be considered a *dramma giocoso*, or humorous drama. (It would seem that history is repeating itself, since grand opera proper grew out of opera buffa.) Rumors have circulated that the New York City Opera has considered staging *Sweeney Todd*, and the Met surprised many with a foray into Broadway's territory by staging *Mahagonny* by Kurt Weill. Critics were not enchanted with this Met experiment, but all performances were sold out.

Opera will continue to mean many things to many people. Through continuous change and development, it will remain a medium of expression on the stage, maintaining its unbroken popularity. For the future, should we look to Broadway and keep an eye on the international houses as well? The next opera evolution may well come from an entirely unexpected source and surprise us all.

CHAPTER TWO

Your first opera

For Adults

Once you have decided that you want to enjoy an opera, you are faced with some decisions. For example, there are over one hundred operas in the standard repertory, a term which means that they are usually performed all of the time all over the world. Which of these should you see first?

A first opera should be chosen for the following qualities: It should be short enough so that it doesn't fatigue and begin to bore the novice. It should have a clear and simple story so that when it is performed in a foreign language, as it usually is, it can be followed easily. It should be rich in melody and full of songs which you will find yourself humming as you walk out of the theater. And it should be colorful and exotic.

There are only a few operas which qualify as ideal for beginners and we list them below in their recommended order.

1. Since its premiere in 1896, *La Bohème*, by Giacomo Puccini, has been the world's most popular opera. It's a heartwarming tale of Bohemian lovers, artistic types starving in a Paris garret, which was once thought quite shocking and dar-

ing, but is now considered charming and romantic. The music is lush and tuneful and it is almost impossible to attend a bad performance of this simple work.

2. *Tosca* is another opera by Puccini with many of the same qualities of *La Bohème*, although the subject of this opera is far more dramatic and violent. Its plot contains the famous "double double-cross," with all of the protagonists dead at the conclusion.

3. *Madama Butterfly*, again by Puccini, is a perennial tearjerker of the Far East with the famous aria, or solo, "Un bel dì" ("One fine day").

4. *Aida*, by the great nineteenth-century Italian composer Giuseppe Verdi, is an excellent introduction to opera although it is longer than any of the above three Puccini works. It is full of pageantry and wonderful sweeping tunes. The opera is set in Egypt, and the celebrated triumphal scene, wherein the Egyptians march on stage with captives and booty, always brings down the house. Often elephants, sometimes confused with the singers, and seminude dancers participate.

5. *Rigoletto*, also by Verdi, is another great favorite with its famous quartet and lovely soprano aria "Caro nome." The theme of *Rigoletto*, set in Renaissance Italy, is sex and revenge, quite easily understood by today's audiences. And those who favor underdogs will be pleased to know that this is one of the few operas in which the baritone instead of the tenor sings the lead role.

6. Verdi's *La Traviata* is another good beginner's opera. It is based on the play *Camille* by Alexandre Dumas *fils*, and many will be familiar with the story through Greta Garbo's 1937 movie. It is one of Verdi's most tuneful and appealing operas.

7. *L'Elisir d'Amore* (*The Elixir of Love*), by Gaetano Donizetti, is a wonderful introduction to opera. It is a short comic opera with some lovely arias by both the soprano and tenor, and, in some productions, a magician comes down in a balloon. *L'Elisir* is great entertainment for the whole family.

8. The always popular *Il Trovatore* is another dramatic work by Verdi. Most audiences will be familiar with the famous

PLATE 4. *Pol Plançon was a suave devil in performances of* Faust *at the turn of the century.* (*Author's collection*)

Anvil Chorus and will enjoy its many marvelous arias, despite the typically violent and convoluted plot.

9. *Carmen*, by Georges Bizet, has been called the perfect opera. It isn't, but it can be the perfect introduction to opera. The trouble is that it must be seen with an excellent singer in the role of Carmen and, unfortunately, excellent Carmens are much rarer than diamonds. *Carmen* seen with an inferior cast can be a crushing bore. But in a good performance the familiar and popular melodies and well-constructed story of this French work give much pleasure.

10. *Faust*, by Charles Gounod, also French, was once the most popular opera in the world and its composer considered the equal of Mozart. Neither is true these days, but even so, *Faust* is a lovely opera with a strong Victorian flavor and stick-to-the-rib melodies. It, too, can be very colorful when presented properly.

Both French operas, *Carmen* and *Faust*, are last on this list for the reason that most singers in the world are trained to sing the Italian repertory and cannot do justice to the very different

French style. Lamentably, this state of things is true even in France.

Other operas which can be recommended for beginners are, in alphabetical order:

Cavalleria Rusticana, by Pietro Mascagni. Italian.
Otello, by Giuseppe Verdi. Italian.
Pagliacci, by Ruggiero Leoncavallo. Italian.
Roméo et Juliette, by Charles Gounod. French.

For Children

Naturally, there are different requirements when taking a child to his or her first opera performance. It is very important that children not be taken to an opera which is long and which might bore them. This will spoil the performance for the rest of the audience temporarily, and opera permanently for the youngster. The drama should be easily followed and especially colorful. It should have strange creatures in exotic costumes. While "love stories" are not good for young audiences, action on the stage will make the opera much more interesting for them. Only the following are recommended:

1. *Hänsel und Gretel,* by Engelbert Humperdinck, the celebrated German composer, has been for years the classic children's opera. It is, of course, the famous fairy tale, complete with wicked witch and children, sung by sopranos, as the protagonists. The music is enchanting. You cannot go wrong with this one.

2. *L'Elisir d'Amore* is a good bet for children, too. The balloon out of the sky and the tenor's drunken scene will be understood and appreciated by them.

3. *Die Zauberflöte* (*The Magic Flute*), by Wolfgang Amadeus Mozart, is a fairy tale with a libretto, or story, which makes little sense to many adult operagoers but which can be very enjoyable for children. It contains a dragon, exotic creatures, a bird catcher in a feathered costume, a benevolent sor-

PLATES 5 AND 6. *Metropolitan Opera productions of* L'Elisir d'Amore (*plate* 5), *and* Hänsel und Gretel (*plate* 6). (*Photos* **courtesy** *Metropolitan Opera press department*)

cerer, an evil sorceress and, naturally, a hopefully handsome
prince and princess. The music is magnificent and moving and
can easily register with children who are already receptive to
the story and stage action.

Operas to Be Avoided

It's of course just as important to avoid a wrong first opera
as it is to find the right one. One mistake can end your experiment with lyric drama. Avoid the long operas with heavy or-
chestration and little melody. Operas with complicated and
subtle plots are inadvisable for the novice, even though these
are often the greatest and ultimately most satisfying operas.
We suggest these be saved for later.

Any opera in the standard repertory which was not recommended for initial viewing must be included in a list of those
to avoid at first.

It is especially important to avoid the Wagnerian operas.
While some of these might have been on the recommended list,
many modern productions all over the world totally ignore the
composer's wishes and make even the most accessible of his operas dull, dark and long. Operas like *Die Walküre, Siegfried,
Das Rheingold* and *Tannhäuser* once meant blazing armor,
flying pennants, flags, dragons, rainbows and picturesque for-
ests. Now there is usually a dark stage, either bare or adorned
with dimly illuminated slabs of rock, if you're lucky, or, if unfortunate, anything in the bizarre imagination of the designer
or director. Fortunately this trend shows signs of reversing itself with the Metropolitan Opera's new production of *Tannhäuser*; but even under ideal circumstances Wagner is rather too
ponderous to be considered a good introduction.

The operas of Richard Strauss are also to be avoided at first.
These can be extremely heavy and cacophonous. Even the
enchanting *Der Rosenkavalier* can sound strange to the novice
operagoer.

Mozart's operas are among the greatest ever written, and in
fact many consider *Don Giovanni* to be the greatest of all.

However, they are not for beginners but for the seasoned listener who will be receptive to their beauty and grandeur. *Die Zauberflöte* is not recommended as a beginning opera for adults, even though for different reasons it is for children. Mozart's most popular opera is probably *Le Nozze di Figaro* (*The Marriage of Figaro*), which is highly recommended (as are indeed all of Mozart's operas) after the beginner has seen some of the suggested first operas.

Mozart's successor, Gioacchino Rossini, wrote many scintillating operas and his overtures to them are very popular. The overture to *William Tell* is especially familiar as it was long the theme music for the once popular *Lone Ranger* radio and television shows. Even his masterpiece, *Il Barbiere di Siviglia* (*The Barber of Seville*), may seem too old-fashioned for some. Like *The Marriage of Figaro*, which is in fact its literary sequel, it is highly recommended after your initial experiences in the opera house.

The incipient operagoer might expect all Puccini and Verdi operas to be suitable for first-time viewing, but this is certainly not so. *Falstaff* was Verdi's last and possibly greatest opera but it is musically far too subtle for the beginner. Puccini's *La Fanciulla del West* (*The Girl of the Golden West*) should have been a natural; set in the American West, replete with cowboys and a lynching, it has flavor and color. Unfortunately, it has little else. Only one tenor aria is worthy of the composer of *La Bohème* and the rest of the music is dry and comparatively devoid of melody. *Turandot* was Puccini's last work. The composer died before finishing it and this fact shows up glaringly in the construction of certain parts of it. Despite an exciting and exotic plot there are several dry and boring sections, and so this too cannot be recommended.

Most operas composed in the twentieth century are known as "modern operas," but what exactly are they? No one is quite sure, but most operagoers are sure that they don't like them. They should never be one's first encounter with opera and indeed should be the very last sampled. Some of the operas in this category are *Pelléas et Mélisande* by Debussy, *Wozzeck* and *Lulu* by Berg, *Peter Grimes* by Britten, *Bomarzo* by Alberto Ginastera, *Jenůfa* by Leoš Janáček and *The Rake's Progress* by Igor Stravinsky, who, incidentally, boasted that he was writing a "Mozart" opera. You may eventually like some or all of these works but please do not begin with them.

If you use the above lists and attend a performance at one of the opera houses we discuss in Chapter Five, with a little luck you will have a marvelous experience, one which will make you want to return again and again.

CHAPTER THREE

Watching an opera

Attending an opera for the first time is an exciting experience. If you have chosen to see a popular opera at a major opera house, your experience is liable to be a very enjoyable one; but there are additional things you can pursue in order to increase your pleasure.

The chances are that whatever opera you have chosen will be performed in a foreign language. Therefore, it is a very good idea to familiarize yourself with the story of the opera before the performance begins. This way you will be able to follow the action reasonably easily and without too much confusion. If you are attending an opera in any American opera house, you can do this right before the performance by reading the plot synopsis in your program. In addition, some people like to read more complete accounts of the plot, available in a number of books, the best of which are listed in Appendix I. Some go even further and read the libretto in an English translation, often on sale in the lobby. This really isn't necessary and can be rather tedious, but it wouldn't hurt to scan a libretto; it can be nice to know at certain times exactly what a singer is saying and singing. While others may even obtain a recording beforehand, it is not such a good idea to form ideas about a work before seeing it in the house for the first time. Eventually the seasoned operagoer begins to pick up some "opera Italian" which adds even more to his or her enjoyment.

Another way to add to your pleasure and receptiveness at a performance is to understand a little of the history and background of the opera you will be watching, something not always discussed in the program. Certainly if one goes to a *Barber of Seville* expecting something along the lines of a Wagnerian opera, there will be at least a shock if not disappointment. There are several good published surveys of opera history that can be useful references to an opera lover, and these too are listed in Appendix I.

In this chapter we will look at the history and background of six of the most popular, but inherently different operas in the repertory. These are operas which feature the schools of verismo, Italian and French grand opera, Wagnerian opera, classical opera buffa, sometimes mistakenly referred to as Mozartean, and opera seria (although, in this instance, actually reformed opera seria). All six works present the listener with different approaches to musical theater. An understanding of these six can prepare the average operagoer with a frame of reference for almost any other opera in the standard repertory.

La Bohème

Today there is little doubt that the world's most popular opera is *La Bohème* by Giacomo Puccini. Many opera directors would despair at the thought of a season without it and the guaranteed full houses it means. It is also the ideal first opera to experience for the very reasons of its popularity. Full of lush, beautiful melodies, it has a very lyrical score abounding with gaiety and humor and the pathos of its tragic ending. The story is a universally appealing and direct one of poor, strug-

gling artists in love, seemingly without a care in the world beyond outwitting the landlord or providing the next meal.

The opera's premiere took place at the Teatro Regio in
Turin, Italy, on February 1, 1896, and was conducted by Ar-
turo Toscanini. Its premiere in the United States was given in
Los Angeles and it was performed at the Metropolitan Opera
House in 1900 with the great Nellie Melba starring as Mimì.
Since then the Met has thrived on *La Bohème* and will soon
give the four hundredth performance of it, a record in the
opera house.

The opera is the most famous example of the verismo
school, the style which flourished during the last part of the
nineteenth century and well into the twentieth. The verists
wanted to write honest, true-to-life stories which told of real
passions and people, and *Bohème*'s story conforms to this
verismo creed. *La Bohème*, from Henri Murger's book of stories *Scènes de la Vie de Bohème*, is based on true characters
with the additional appeal that it is the story of student life in
the Latin Quarter of Paris in the mid-nineteenth century.
Today we may view the story as a charming evocation of a nostalgic era, but when *La Bohème* was first presented the opera
was considered shockingly contemporary. The love affair between the unmarried protagonists was viewed by some as im-
moral and unworthy of the traditions of grand opera. Even the
critics prophesied early doom for this opera. Most of them,
however, lived to see it firmly established as the favorite it is to
this day.

La Bohème is probably Puccini's finest opera. Although not
as purely dramatic as the later *Tosca*, nor as musically sophisticated as *Madama Butterfly* or *Turandot*, it crystallizes the
very best that Puccini has to offer without being guilty of senti-
mentality or overstatement. It is one of the easiest of the
foreign-language operas for an English-speaking audience to
enjoy, as its admirably simple story and unsubtle action can be
grasped without difficulty. It is also incredibly durable, in that
it can withstand being seen dozens of times without becoming
hackneyed or boring. And Puccini's tunes never fail to work
their magic.

One of the traits of a verismo opera is that it usually doesn't waste any time getting on with the action—it's a compact affair with no excess fat. No exception, *La Bohème* begins with a very short overture that effectively sets the tone. This short prelude, the "Bohemians' theme," recurring throughout the opera, raises the curtain on Rodolfo, the tenor, and his baritone friend, Marcello, in their large, bare garret. Rodolfo is trying to keep warm while Marcello works on his painting. Here the music is light and cheery while the two friends banter back and forth. To keep warm, Rodolfo has just burned his new play in the stove when Colline, a basso, enters. Then the fourth member of the group, Schaunard, also a baritone, enters with two errand boys who are unexpectedly carrying food, wine and firewood. In the midst of their playful, joyous repast the landlord knocks on the door demanding his rent. The Bohemians turn their high spirits on the poor man until they have tricked him into leaving without his sous. This comic scene establishes the mood of the opera through Act Two.

When the laughing friends decide to go on along to the Café Momus, Rodolfo lingers, telling his friends he will be down in a moment. No sooner have they departed than there is a knock on the garret door. It is a young girl from next door, Mimì, the soprano, who has come to beg a light for her candle. Seeing her fainting and coughing from weakness and hunger, Rodolfo asks her to sit awhile as he lights her candle. Mimì, shy with this handsome young man, starts to leave but she finds that she has dropped her key. In this most charming scene they both grope for the key, but as Rodolfo touches her hand, he forgets about the key. Then begins one of the most celebrated sequences of arias and duet in all of opera. The young people are simply introducing themselves, but in the language of the beautiful verismo music, they are beginning to fall in love. Rodolfo exclaims about her cold hand. This is the lyrical tenor aria "Che gelida manina," or "What a cold little hand." Mimì answers him shyly with "Mi chiamano Mimì," or "My name is Mimì," music swelling, then ending on a quiet note. After a little awkward conversation in which Rodolfo calls to his friends belowstairs that he will be bringing someone to the café, Rodolfo, the poet, sings of the moonlight on her face, "O soave fanciulla," or "O, lovely maiden." Their voices uniting in a passionate song, this duet truly begins their romance. The duet and the act end as they leave the stage, Mimì singing a final high C in a fading, dreamy manner.

This simple first act is true verismo. The conversation is very natural and realistic, with the boisterous Bohemians acting as Puccini and many of his artistic friends may have done in their struggling youths. Still, there are quite conventional operatic devices here. "Che gelida manina" and "Mi chiamano Mimì" are true set pieces, or arias. However, they are skillfully woven into the act so that they do not seem unnatural or disruptive. The duet "O soave fanciulla" is another set piece, also woven into the fabric of the music so that it becomes simply the heady conversation of young love. These three pieces are a feast of lovely music for the opera lover; rarely does an opera deliver so much melody in so short a space of time.

Act Two is all fun and high spirits. We see the Café Momus center stage amid the bustle of the waiters and a happy crowd of patrons. This is a wonderfully nostalgic French sidewalk café in the heart of the Latin Quarter on Christmas Eve. Children, shoppers, vendors and other colorful characters wander the streets shouting, cheering and laughing in holiday celebration. All of this is colorfully reflected in the boisterous music, with snatches of chorus and recitative. Very little dramatic action occurs in this act, although it serves to emphasize the carefree, happy life of the Bohemians and further cement the new love affair of Rodolfo and Mimì. Most importantly, we are introduced to a new character, Marcello's girl friend Musetta, the coquette, sung by a soprano. She has come to the café with a prosperous new "friend." Taunting Marcello as he drinks with his friends, the flirtatious Musetta sings her famous "Waltz," then sends her elderly admirer away on a pretext. Marcello has scarcely needed this provocation to become jealous; but after a brief squabble, he and Musetta are reconciled. Before the end of the act, Musetta has managed to trick her "friend" into paying the bill as the Bohemians join the gay, noisy crowd.

PLATE 7. *The Metropolitan Opera production of* La Bohème *featured this lovely winter scene for Act III. (Photo courtesy Metropolitan Opera press department)*

"Musetta's Waltz" is the one real aria in this last unrelievedly happy act in the opera; the rest of the music is taken up with ensemble and chorus singing interspersed with recitative. Boisterous and carefree, the music tells the story of this act.

Act Three immediately reveals the sign of things to come. It opens on a peaceful dawn snow scene near one of the gates of Paris. The Bohemians can be heard singing in a little inn which sports one of Marcello's paintings as a signboard. The music has a gentle quality and a slight touch of melancholy despite the sounds of celebration from the tavern. Mimì enters through the gate coughing and shivering. Hesitantly, she inquires for Marcello. When Marcello comes out to persuade Mimì to join the celebrating Bohemians, she refuses, crying that she is tired of Rodolfo's jealousy. Marcello advises her to leave Rodolfo. Suddenly Rodolfo himself appears and Mimì hides in the shadows to listen. To Marcello, Rodolfo complains of Mimì, of her flirtations and constant cough which actually worries him; he too wants a separation. Overhearing Rodolfo's concern, realizing that she is really seriously ill, Mimì weeps in her dark corner. Her coughing reveals her hiding place and

Mimì bids Rodolfo a sad farewell after Marcello reenters the inn. Her beautiful aria "Addio senza rancor," or "Farewell with no ill will," is followed by a duet accented by the sounds of a violent quarrel between Marcello and Musetta as they leave the tavern. The lovely duet becomes a quartet, with a witty, piquant contrast between the two couples. Recalling their past happiness, Mimì and Rodolfo agree to put off their parting until the spring. Although the curtain falls on their reconciliation, there has been a foreshadowing of the final act, the tragic denouement of this simple tale.

The musical theme which throughout the opera has stood for the Bohemians opens Act Four. Once again Rodolfo and Marcello are alone in their garret, seemingly happy and hard at work. Each tells the other of seeing his lover with someone else. Though they are skeptical, the laughter is rather forced. Rodolfo's little song about Mimì, "O Mimì, tu più non torni," or "O Mimì, you return no longer," becomes an emotional duet with Marcello about their lost loves. Into the carefree lives of the Bohemians has crept a new sadness. As before, the entrance of their friends Schaunard and Colline with food cheers them. As this feverish celebration reaches a crescendo of dancing and joking, the door bursts open and in rushes Musetta to say that Mimì is outside, exhausted from climbing the stairs. When Rodolfo and Marcello assist Mimì into the garret and place her on the bed, she asks weakly for a muff for her cold hands, a sad reminder of her cold hands in the first act. There is a scramble for money. Musetta removes her earrings with orders to Marcello to sell them and buy medicine. Colline takes off his beloved coat and in a philosophical aria sings farewell to it, a rare basso aria by Puccini, "Vecchia zimarra," or "Old robe." The others go out, leaving Mimì and Rodolfo alone, and the orchestra repeats many of the melodies which were heard in happier times. Mimì and Rodolfo sing, recalling past happiness. She is wracked by coughing as Musetta, Marcello and Schaunard return, then seems to fall asleep, holding the muff that Musetta has brought to her. Simply, quietly, the music prepares us for the end, as Colline also returns. Marcello and Schaunard are the first to see that Mimì

has died and turn pityingly to Rodolfo. "Coraggio," Marcello
comforts him as Rodolfo flings himself on Mimì's lifeless form
with a heartrending cry of "Mimì! Mimì!"

The opera ends with a sad reprise of an earlier theme Mimì
has sung. This ending, which is simple and straightforward, is
one of the most moving in opera and there is rarely a dry eye
in the house when the curtain comes down. The quiet of the
music before Rodolfo realizes that Mimì has died is excruciat-
ing in its dramatic power.

La Bohème is relatively short and full of unornamented
melodies, but it is surprisingly subtle. Although it's a very simple tale of boy meets girl, boy loses girl, boy gets girl back only
to lose her forever, it goes far deeper as we laugh and suffer
with the poor Bohemian artists.

As mentioned before, the opera is based on the popular stories of Henri Murger. Puccini's contemporary Ruggiero Leoncavallo, who wrote the well-loved Pagliacci, also wrote a version of La Bohème, and since then there have been a few
movies made of the same story; but none of these has survived
and flourished as has Puccini's masterpiece.

Although not "grand," La Bohème is quintessentially operatic. The story could have been told so effectively only in operatic form. The story and the music have been welded so well
together that it is today almost impossible to think of Bohemians without Puccini's music.

Faust

For many years before La Bohème made its appearance, and
for many years after, the world's most popular opera was Faust
by Charles Gounod. The Metropolitan Opera gave so many
performances of it that the New York Sun critic William J.
Henderson dubbed the Met the "Faustspielhaus," a pun on
the Bayreuth Festspielhaus. The Met's casts, including the legendary tenor Jean de Reszke, along with Pol Plançon and
Emma Eames, or Nellie Melba and Jean Lassalle, made it the
hottest ticket of the day. Written in 1859, the opera made

PLATE 8. *An amusing cartoon of* 1899 *showing the regard composers enjoyed at the turn of the century. Note Gounod's high position among them.* (Author's collection)

Gounod the most famous composer of his time and it was common for the critics and public to regard him as a master the equal of Mozart and Beethoven. *Faust* remained popular for many years and only the recent lack of good singers of French style has caused it to fall somewhat from its high pedestal. Today *Faust* is enjoying a resurgence in popularity; a brief look explains its ever present charm.

Faust is a classic example of French grand opera of the Belle Époque. Full of melody and dramatic action, *Faust* can be as effective as any opera and more entertaining than many when properly performed.

After a tuneful overture containing many of the opera's famous melodies, the curtain rises on old Dr. Faust in his study. He sings a long tenor solo poring over his dusty tomes, regretting that with all of his knowledge he still doesn't know the riddle of life. In his despair, he contemplates suicide. The sounds of young people outside recall his own youth to him and in a burst of desperation he calls upon Satan. "Me voici," booms Méphistophélès, the basso, as he magically materializes from a dark corner of the room. In a stirring duet they make the standard pact: youth and wealth in exchange for Faust's soul. But Faust hesitates and the devil, usually elegantly clad as a debonair, rakish gentleman (although he sometimes sports a tail), conjures up a vision of the beautiful Marguerite at her spinning wheel. Upon this enticement Faust swears and the two sing exuberantly, Méphistophélès on the acquisition of a soul and Faust to see that he has metamorphosed into a dashing, handsome young man.

Act Two opens in the midst of the kermess, or German village fair. In the nearby inn the crowds sing happily. Valentin, the brave soldier, a baritone, and his young friend Siebel, a role sung by a mezzo-soprano in a man's costume, join the crowd. In the famous baritone aria "Avant de quitter," or "Before departing," Valentin prays that, when he is gone to war, heaven will protect his sister Marguerite. This lovely aria has long been a popular favorite because of its noble, sweeping grandeur. Gounod's melodies are as deceptively simple as Puccini's, but the orchestral scoring and emphasis are slightly different; as in "Avant de quitter," elegance and refinement are more important elements than power of delivery. Amid the revelry, Méphistophélès interrupts another singer named Wagner (no relation to the composer) to sing the cynical "Le veau d'or," a blasphemous song of the golden calf. The crowd becomes horrified as after his song he makes wine flow from an empty cask. When he dares to toast Marguerite with this brew, Valentin draws his sword, which Méphistophélès magically breaks. Realizing that it is the devil among them, the crowd raise the hilts of their swords to ward him off with these makeshift crosses and their magnificent, harmonious chant. Méphistophélès cringes away. The musical transition of the chorus from drunken revelry to pious horror is extremely effective.

The kermess festivities return to merry singing and dancing. Marguerite demurely crosses the stage and Faust takes this opportunity to approach her. The music is rapturous here, but Marguerite declines Faust's offer to escort her home. The waltz resumes in a mad frenzy as the curtain is lowered.

In this act we have the essence of Gounod. One memorable tune follows another while medieval color and drama whirl on the stage. Yet, when Marguerite comes on stage for her brief appearance, everything else seems to stop and focus on her and she must command our interest and sympathy with her few crucial lines, an effective but difficult entrance for the soprano. It is of course imperative for the singers, especially Méphistophélès, to remain Gallic and elegant and to refrain from "hamming." This keeps the drama from seeming hokey against the background of the dancing, reveling crowds.

Act Three, the most famous in the opera, features the celebrated Garden Scene. On stage is Marguerite's cottage and garden. Siebel wanders in to sing his naïve "Flower Song." After Siebel leaves a bouquet, a love token for Marguerite, Faust appears with Méphistophélès. The devil leaves Faust alone on stage in order to fetch a companion to the flowers that Siebel has left. Faust lovingly admires the cottage and sings the beautiful "Salut, demeure," or "All hail, thou dwelling," a tenor aria which has as its main accompaniment a lovely violin obbligato. Although an ancestor of La Bohème's "Che gelida

manina," "Salut, demeure" demands refinement and purity of
line in the singer's delivery, and the final high note should be
taken softly, lyrically, lovingly, as opposed to the full volume it
usually receives.

Méphistophélès returns to the garden with a casket of jewels
which he places near Siebel's homely bouquet. The plotting
pair then retire as Marguerite enters to sit at her spinning
wheel, singing a simple old song about "The King of Thule."
Her song suddenly turns to thoughts of the handsome stranger,
Faust; then, spotting the ornate casket, she opens it with
delight and amazement. She cannot resist trying the costly
jewels on and admiring herself in the mirror she has found in
the box as she sings her most difficult aria of the opera. This is
the famous "Jewel Song," which begins with a burst of coloratura and trills. Her neighbor Martha, a bumbling old woman
(or, rather, a mezzo-soprano made to look like one!), enters
and is also drawn to the fabulous jewelry. Méphistophélès
comes in to draw the inconvenient Martha away as Faust
approaches Marguerite. As they promenade around the garden
they sing the "Garden Scene Quartet." With this quartet there
begins one long unbroken stream of melody of a very sensuous
nature. Here Gounod has actually composed a long musical se-
duction. Martha disappears with the dashing Méphistophélès,
whose "Invocation" calls upon the night to cast its spell over
the lovers. Faust sings of his love to the naïve, innocent Marguerite, who still resists his entreaties. She breaks from his embrace and runs into the cottage. Méphistophélès taunts Faust
not to wait for the morning, and, as he has foretold, Marguerite opens her window to sing of her rapture to the stars.
Faust rushes to her, she can no longer resist him and her seduc-
tion is reflected in the sensuous music as Méphistophélès
laughs with evil triumphant glee.

The next scene features Marguerite alone in her room in despair and is often omitted due to the length of the opera. Most
productions skip to the church scene. Here alone and shunned
by all, Marguerite seeks solace in the cathedral as the curtain
rises on Act Four. When she lifts her voice in despairing
prayer, she is answered by the powerful, menacing tones of

Méphistophélès that she is doomed to the infernal regions, "À toi l'enfer," in a most effective basso display.

The next scene takes place in the square in front of the cathedral. Another of the opera's famous tunes, which once made organ grinders and music box manufacturers very happy, is the "Soldiers' Chorus" announcing that the war is over and the men are home. Valentin leaves his troops and turns home, but outside, Méphistophélès, followed by Faust, taunts him with his mocking serenade, "Vous qui faites l'endormie," or "You who pretend to be sleeping." Valentin angrily bursts from the cottage, sword in hand, to avenge the honor of his sister. Valentin challenges Faust, who is suffering from remorse and shame. In an exciting trio Méphistophélès uses his magic to help Faust kill Valentin and the guilty pair run off stage, leaving Valentin dying. The dying soldier curses Marguerite when she rushes to him. Great baritones, like the fabled Victor Maurel, made a tremendous dramatic effect with this awesomely tragic moment. As Valentin dies, Marguerite weeps uncontrollably.

The first scene of Act Five is the Walpurgis Night Ballet. As was fashionable in nineteenth-century French grand opera, it takes place in a late act. The orgies of ghosts and demons take place to some of Gounod's most sensuous music. Méphistophélès tries to beguile Faust with the ghosts of Cleopatra, Helen of Troy, Phryne and others, but suddenly Marguerite appears in a vision and the remorseful Faust demands that Méphistophélès take him to her. This is a prime example of opera ballet: drama and pantomime to brilliant, vivid music. The ballet orgy should not be crude, but an unholy swirl of ghosts and demons in frenzied ballet. It's an excellent opportunity for a good choreographer and can be one of the highlights of the opera. Sometimes the scene and/or the ballet is altogether omitted or badly cut, but it really is of dramatic importance since there is a need for a separation in time before the next scene.

Scene Two is the finale of the opera, and though short, it contains some of the most beautiful music. Méphistophélès brings Faust to Marguerite in her prison cell, where she awaits

execution for the murder of her illegitimate child. Faust tries
to convince the distraught Marguerite to flee with them, but is
appalled to find her delirious, singing the tunes of the happy
days of the kermess and her garden. Upon the devil's impatient
call to hurry, she comes to her senses and in a passage of
religious purity refutes both Faust and Méphistophélès in horror. As she dies with the hope of heaven and forgiveness
Méphistophélès triumphantly calls for her judgment.
"Jugée," or "Condemned," he sings, but an angelic chorus
replies that she is saved. To soul-stirring chords in the orchestra, Faust is dragged to his infernal doom by his diabolic
master. This trio is one of the greatest finales in opera and
never fails to bring down the house no matter how well or
poorly it is sung. The last resonant chords of music are always
drowned out in the enthusiastic applause.

Fastidious Germans have often objected to *Faust* on the
basis that it is a popular, simplified version of the great masterpiece by Goethe. Although very popular in Germany it is tact-
fully entitled *Margarethe*. While, of course, the story is a pale
approximation of the greatness of the Goethe poem, *Faust* is
still one of the most effective opera plots with its contest between sensuous pleasure and religious piety. Beyond the stirring moral lesson and the ardent love story, it presents an unusual amount of real action on stage and an extremely satisfying
musical experience.

Aida

Mention grand opera to someone and the chances are that
he or she will think of *Aida* by Giuseppe Verdi. Above all else,
Aida is indeed grand. Opera companies like to pull out all
stops when producing it, using countless extras, the full chorus
and maybe a few elephants. This pageantry never fails to
enthrall audiences, and many travelers to Italy count the lavish
production of *Aida* at the ancient Baths of Caracalla in Rome
as one of their travel highlights. For many years *Aida* was the
signature work of the Metropolitan Opera and used to be syn-

onymous with such names as Caruso, Toscanini, Emmy Destinn, Elisabeth Rethberg, Giovanni Martinelli and other legendary stars. Many feel that it was Caruso in the role of Radames who made the opera so popular in the United States.

Aida was written at the request of the Khedive of Egypt, Ismail Pasha, who wanted a grand opera on an Egyptian subject to celebrate the opening of the Suez Canal. Although another Verdi opera, *Rigoletto*, was actually performed for the opening in 1869, *Aida* received its premiere in Cairo in 1871. At the time it was regarded as the crowning achievement of the distinguished career of a great composer, for Verdi was fifty-eight years old and had made it plain that he did not plan to follow it with another opera. In retrospect, however, *Aida* is in fact only the first of the three great masterpieces of his "mature" period. *Aida*, *Otello* and finally *Falstaff* represent a great stride for that giant of Italian opera. The rich scoring, the subtle harmonies and advanced modulation combined with a total mastery of dramatic music have made these operas cornerstones of the popular operatic repertory. Of the three, *Aida* is the most popular due to the melodious score and a story which, set against the backdrop of the romantic grandeur of ancient Egypt, enables us to become very involved with the protagonists.

The prelude immediately places us in ancient Egypt. Really a miniature tone poem, with a certain stylistic debt to the works of Wagner, the musical imagery transcends the Italian form. The curtain rises on a scene in the palace of the Egyptian Pharaoh. The all-powerful high priest, Ramfis, a basso, tells Radames, the tenor hero, that the Ethiopian army is threatening the Egyptian borders. Following a brief recitative in which he daydreams of great deeds at arms, Radames sings his most famous aria, "Celeste Aida," or "Heavenly Aida," a love song to the slave girl Aida. This aria should be sung with a rapt and dreamy quality and not at all shouted, as it is commonly attacked today. The high note, which is sung at full volume usually to make points for the tenor, is much more effective when sung as the composer wanted, piano, or quietly. But few tenors are able or willing to try such a controlled, difficult

feat. When they do the audience, used to the loud note, sometimes feels cheated. Beyond this, it is surely one of the most
difficult moments in opera for a tenor, for he must sing a
major and strenuous aria with little warm-up.

Now enters Amneris, the daughter of the Pharaoh, who is in
love with Radames. She is shortly followed by Aida, the slave
girl and, all unsuspected, the daughter of the King of Ethiopia.
Watching Aida and Radames jealously, Amneris, sung by a
mezzo-soprano, guesses that the two are in love. The Pharaoh
enters with his entourage as a messenger reports that the
Ethiopians are nearing Thebes. Radames is charged with leading the Egyptian army to meet this threat and to stirring, martial music all leave the stage except Aida, who is torn by
conflicting emotions. Carried away by her love for Radames,
Aida, the soprano, has joined the crowd in singing, "Ritorna
vincitor!" or "Return victorious!" But she is the princess of
Ethiopia, and torn between her loyalties, she now sings a melancholy aria of despair.

In the brief scene which follows, the priests bless Radames
and his army. The chorus of priests and priestesses and their rit-
ualistic procession evoke the ancient world.

Act Two begins in the luxurious apartments of Amneris. She
cruelly abuses her slave girl Aida, whom she has tricked into
admitting her love for Radames. Amneris threatens her with
death as we hear the swell of a triumphal march in celebration
of Radames' victory over the Ethiopians.

The scene changes to the great Triumphal Procession, one
of the most celebrated chorus and ensemble scenes in all of
opera. The King and, it would appear, all of Egypt are there
singing, "Glory to Egypt!" Dancing girls perform an exotic
ballet followed by a procession of soldiers, chariots and banners
to a stirring march.

Radames enters in a horse-drawn chariot amid the admiring
throng and is embraced by his King, who calls him the savior
of the country. In his gratitude, the Pharaoh offers Radames
anything he desires. But first the prisoners are brought in,
among them Amonasro, unrecognized as the King of the
Ethiopians. Aida rushes to her father's side but he commands

her to keep his rank a secret from the Egyptians. Amonasro convincingly explains to the crowd that he saw the Ethiopian King die in battle. Radames now asks as his favor the freedom of the captives, but this Ramfis and the other priests object to and the Pharaoh declares that Aida and Amonasro will be kept as hostages while the other prisoners are set free. As Radames' reward, the Pharaoh decides to give him Amneris' hand in marriage. There follows one of the great ensembles in opera, through which the characters express their differing emotions: Amonasro, revenge; Amneris, pride and happiness; Aida, despair; and Radames, the thought that all of Egypt is not worth the love of Aida; all against the swelling chorus of Pharaoh, priests and populace singing to the glory of Egypt and its gods.

The Act Three curtain rises on the banks of the Nile, with an amazing overture that seems the very essence of the Nile itself. The pizzicato of the strings and the melody of oboe and bassoon conjure up visions of reeds, river bugs and even a mummy or two. The chorus of priests is heard praying to the goddess Isis as Aida appears. She sings the great "O patria mia," or "My native land," as she waits for Radames, in which she sings of her happy childhood in Ethiopia. Amonasro interrupts her reverie and compels her with accusations of treason to use her influence with Radames to find out through which pass the Egyptians will be marching so the regrouped Ethiopians can attack them. He hides as Radames approaches singing "Pur ti riveggo, mia dolce Aida," or "Again I see you, my dear Aida." She asks that he prove his love by fleeing with her. He resists but using her most enticing charms, Aida persuades him and then tricks him into revealing the situation of the Egyptian army. At this vital disclosure Amonasro gleefully shows himself and reveals himself as the King of the Ethiopians. Radames realizes how he has been tricked, but it is too late, for Amneris has overheard them and has summoned help. Radames is arrested while Amonasro and Aida manage to escape. The Nile scene closes with Radames' noble declaration, "Io resto a te," or "I surrender."

Through the great aria for soprano, two duets and the brief ensemble finale, the musical and dramatic tension is maintained on a very high level. It is worthy of note that Aida must ascend to a high C in a very exposed way during her duet with Radames. A cruelly demanding note which many sopranos, including the marvelous Rosa Ponselle, have dreaded, it occurs when she urges Radames to fly with her, "Fuggiam, fuggiam!"

At the start of Act Four Amneris, alone in the King's palace, grieves over Radames' fate which the priests are at that moment deliberating. She demands that he be brought to her and offers to plead for him if he will forget the slave girl and love her, Amneris. But he refuses her offer, pledging his eternal love for Aida. Amneris is determined on revenge. We watch her on stage, suffering as she listens to the priests questioning Radames. Amneris' agony as Radames refuses, off stage with the priests, to answer their questions is dramatic in the extreme. He is declared "Traditor," or "Traitor," and is sentenced to be buried alive in a tomb (over sixty years before the same fate was suffered by Boris Karloff in *The Mummy*). Tortured by this grim sentence, Amneris curses the priests to whom she had denounced the man she loves.

The final scene features a set split between two horizontal levels. The upper level is the interior of the Temple of Vulcan at Memphis and the lower one a deep, dark vault. Radames is sealed into his burial vault with a huge stone. Resigned to his own fate, his thoughts turn to his beloved Aida. But he is not alone, for Aida herself has hidden in the tomb to die with her lover. They sing a beautiful farewell to earth, "O terra addio," resigned to eternity together. In the temple above them, Amneris joins their song, mournful, repentant.

Aida is a very difficult opera to cast. The title role demands a cross between a full dramatic and a lyric soprano. Such a singer is referred to as a spinto, an uncommon range. The tenor role presents similar difficulties. The Golden Age tenor Jean de Reszke would often not even sing "Celeste Aida," as too taxing, coming as it does at the beginning of the opera. Besides, his fans in high society came fashionably late and would have missed it anyway! Beyond these vocal considerations, the opera is as demanding on a conductor as any major symphonic work; the Triumphal Scene is a major challenge. Yet it has been observed, *Aida* is a no-fail proposition: even a minor company with small resources can give an effective if inexpensive production because there is so much inherent grandeur in the music. And when a big company puts the right singers and sets on stage, ancient Egypt comes to life as in perhaps no other reincarnation.

Tannhäuser

The operas of Richard Wagner represent the culmination of German romanticism. All have several things in common: rather than using contemporary libretti, they are based on old German myths and legends or, as in the case of *Tannhäuser* and *Die Meistersinger*, on a combination of legend and historical fact. Wagner was fascinated with the struggle between Christianity and pagan mythology and in some of his operas he explored this struggle. His music dramas, as he called them, were written and composed by himself with no collaborator or librettist. The music is brilliantly orchestrated and of a very heavy symphonic nature. It is also very sensuous and full of another of his innovations, leitmotiv or theme. This was Wagner's device of using a theme to conjure up a character or event or mood. The music is very difficult vocally and many singers have specialized in Wagnerian opera, as its demands are virtually unique. Singers for this music must have large voices and great stamina, for the acts are long with extended stretches of singing and little rest for the performers. Many of Wagner's operas can seem very heavy to the listener at first and it's a good idea to approach them through one of his more accessible works, the earlier works which follow more traditional modes than the later ones which represent a total departure. Of these most accessible operas, which also include *Lohengrin* and the later *Die Meistersinger*, we will look at the opera which gave Wagner much of his early fame and popularity, not to mention quite a bit of infamy in Paris.

Tannhäuser is based on several common legends, one of which held that in medieval times the ancient gods had retreated to the underworld, and Germans felt that Venus in particular was conveniently close by in a German mountain, which became known as the Venusberg. According to old legends, the sensuous knight Tannhäuser was reputed to be well connected with Venus.

The overture is the longest and most complicated of the operas we have looked at so far. It opens with the leitmotiv of the beautiful "Pilgrims' Chorus." As it fades, the "Venus theme" becomes stronger and more riotous until it is again subdued by the "Pilgrims' theme." This is of course a microcosm of the entire opera, in which a Christian knight is led into sin and then saved by his faith. The overture is of such stirring magnificence that it has been a staple in concert programs ever since its composition.

The version of this opera we will discuss here is the second, or "Paris" version, as opposed to the "Dresden," or first version. For the Paris version Wagner added a ballet at the beginning of the first scene, known as the "Parisian Bacchanale." As Tannhäuser lounges by the side of Venus, sung by a mezzo-soprano, in her subterranean court, she amuses him with pagan and mythical dances. Through the ballet she conjures up the "Rape of Europa," "Leda and the Swan" and other lecherous myths. Tannhäuser, however, has become bored by it all and wants to return to his life on earth. He sings his famous tenor "Hymn to Venus" only to long distractedly for his past life. When Venus warns him that his return would only mean trouble he answers that he has faith in Mary. At the name of the Virgin Mary, Venus and her court magically disappear, leaving Tannhäuser alone near a castle in a valley of the Wartburg.

The beauty of the earth is immediately apparent in the music of a shepherd boy, sung by a soprano. The pure innocence of the shepherd's song is accompanied by an exquisite oboe obbligato and the chorus of passing pilgrims in a musical combination of fantastic beauty, a combination not often found in Italian opera. Overcome by emotion, Tannhäuser falls to his knees in prayer. Hunting horns are heard as the ruler of the region, the Landgrave, and a group of minnesingers come up the path. This is a historic element to the

legend; the minnesingers were singing nobles who wrote poetry and songs during the middle ages in Germany. The party joyously greets the long-absent Tannhäuser and asks him where he has been, to which he gives evasive answers. He plans to wander on but his baritone friend, the minstrel knight Wolfram, reminds him of his true love, Elisabeth, the Landgrave's niece, who has sorely missed him. Moved, Tannhäuser will go with them.

Act Two begins in the hall of minstrels in the Wartburg castle. Preparations have been made for a song contest when Elisabeth, the soprano, enters with a salute to the hall in her joyful aria "Dich, teure Halle," or "Hail, hall of song." Wolfram enters with Tannhäuser and the two lovers sing a duet in praise of the miracle which has reunited them. The Landgrave enters, then to a magnificent march the rest of the court appears with a swelling chorus of greeting.

The Landgrave welcomes them and names "love" as the theme of the contest. The minnesingers sing of virtuous love, but Tannhäuser sings of the delights of sensualism. Finally he breaks into his "Hymn to Venus" as if hypnotized. The women flee in horror and the men draw swords when Elisabeth intercedes for her unfaithful lover. Hearing the noble pilgrims' chorus outside, the repentant Tannhäuser rushes off to join them in their pilgrimage to Rome.

The lovely prelude to Act Three is made up of many of the themes heard throughout the opera, including "Elisabeth's Intercession," "Tannhäuser's Agony" and "Repentance" and subordinate themes of the "Pilgrims' Chorus" and "Forgiveness."

Act Three opens in the Wartburg valley, in which Elisabeth is seen kneeling and praying before a shrine to the Virgin. In the distance the chorus of the pilgrims heralds their return from Rome. Elisabeth watches in vain for Tannhäuser. She falls again to her knees and sings her lovely plea to the Virgin Mary known as "Elisabeth's Prayer."

Wolfram watches as she rises and makes her sorrowful return to the castle. Night has fallen and, alone on stage, Wolfram sings of the shining star in the valley and the lovely Elisabeth. This beautiful and moving lyrical baritone aria, "O du mein holder Abendstern," or "O evening star," is one reason for the opera's lasting popularity.

To a gloomy motive in the orchestra, Tannhäuser all but drags himself on stage and relates to Wolfram the Pope's refusal to pardon him. Tannhäuser's salvation will come only when the Pope's staff bears leaves, in other words, never. He asks the way to the Venusberg, where he seeks only forgetfulness. At this, Venus reappears and the sensuous Venusberg theme is played as she holds out her arms in welcome. But Wolfram names Elisabeth once again to Tannhäuser and, as he muses on that name, Venus vanishes for good. The bells mournfully toll, for the faithful Elisabeth has died. To the music of her funeral train, the mourners appear with her bier. Overcome with grief and despair, Tannhäuser falls dying beside her. A second group of pilgrims enters, bearing the Pope's staff, which has borne green leaves. By this miracle Tannhäuser's soul is saved.

This moving work has many conventional arias, such as

Wolfram's "O evening star," "Elisabeth's Prayer" and Tann-häuser's "Hymn to Venus," but the Wagnerisms of broad leit-motivs and heavily scored orchestral passages, often accompa-nying long duets and ensembles, are in strong evidence. The dramatic conflict between paganism and Christian ideals is clearly outlined by the psychological themes of the music. The great beauty of the score is irresistible and Wagner's innovative genius has combined it with a sweeping representation of Ger-man romanticism.

Don Giovanni

As great as are the operas we have examined, I believe that the greatest of all is *Don Giovanni* by Wolfgang Amadeus Mozart. It is the great operatic masterpiece of the man many consider the supreme composer of Western music, a master of every musical form, including symphonic, liturgical, chamber, solo instrumental and, naturally, his preferred form, opera. Since its premiere in Prague in 1787, *Don Giovanni* has been subject to countless interpretations and arguments concerning its meaning. It is classified as a *dramma giocoso*, which means a comic opera with some serious episodes; but this has satisfied no one and it is argued to this day whether or not *Don Gio-vanni* is tragedy or comedy. Among the theatrical repertory only Shakespeare's *Hamlet* has been the subject of more discussion and interpretation, and that only because it was written centu-ries earlier.

Don Giovanni was an immediate hit in Prague, a city much more receptive to Mozart's genius than was Vienna, and quickly spread throughout the world. The story of Don Juan and his fiery punishment is an old one, used by many drama-tists and composers, including the great playwright Molière. The story was no doubt very familiar to the audiences which first saw the opera and they were probably quite ready to ac-cept it as a comedy, but the dawning of German romanticism caused it to be almost immediately reexamined by such author-ities as E. T. A. Hoffmann, famed for his bizarre short stories, among others and the argument has been on ever since. In reality, *Don Giovanni* is a classic example of the opera buffa form. It was not a form Mozart invented (a form which some critics who examine the works of such contemporaries as Giovanni Paisiello, Domenico Cimarosa and Joseph Haydn falsely label "Mozartean"), but the standard form of the period which Mozart brought to the greatest height of accomplishment. *Don Giovanni* is so complex, so profound and so full of grandeur that it is sometimes hard to remember that it is really a comedy. The fact that Mozart brilliantly parodied certain opera seria conventions has only confused the matter further for some.

The opera was commissioned by the manager of the Prague opera house, who wanted something to follow the great success Mozart's *Le Nozze di Figaro* had achieved there. No doubt Mozart and his librettist Lorenzo da Ponte began by trying to produce a work of a similar nature. Yet, with the assistance of that brilliant rogue da Ponte, and the collaboration of a real-life Don Juan, Casanova himself, Mozart followed up the phenomenal *Nozze* with the more complex *Don*.

A standard eighteenth-century opera buffa, *Don Giovanni* is composed of classic set pieces, arias, duets and ensembles, strung between recitative, or sung declamation. The opera takes place in two acts, but each is quite long, with five scenes in Act One and five scenes plus an epilogue in the second. An opera house is fully extended to meet the challenge and provide the necessary scene changes quickly enough.

The overture begins on a somber note but brightens quickly and ends in a truly comic vein. On stage, in the garden of Donna Anna's palace, is Leporello, the servant of Don Giovanni, a role usually played by a basso buffo, or comic bass. The funniest lines in the opera fall to Leporello, who is not in the least awed by his famous master. At present awaiting his master, he sings "Notte e giorno," or "Working night and day." A struggle interrupts his complaints. Don Giovanni, sung by either a bass or a baritone, appears dragging the resisting Donna Anna by one hand and hiding his face in his cloak with the other. Her father, the Commendatore, appears at her screams. Donna Anna escapes into the palace, leaving the reluctant Don to face the outraged old nobleman. Their short sword fight ends with the death of the Commendatore. Here the orchestra stops playing while Don Giovanni and Leporello converse to the accompaniment of a keyboard instrument, a device know as *secco* recitative. Leporello asks, "Chi è morto, voi o il vecchio?" or "Who's dead, you or the old man?" This sarcasm following the death of the Commendatore certainly mitigates the tragic nature of the opera.

The Don and Leporello flee as Donna Anna reappears with her fiancé, the tenor Don Ottavio, to rescue her father. They discover his dead body and express their horror in *secco* recitative. Swearing vengeance, Donna Anna, sung by a dramatic soprano, begins a *recitativo accompagnato*, or recitative to full orchestral accompaniment. Don Ottavio joins her in a stirring duet.

Scene Two finds Leporello and Don Giovanni conversing on a road near Seville. To Leporello's reproaches, Don Giovanni returns an imperious command for silence. The Don tells Leporello of his latest conquest and the irrepressible Leporello requests more information so he can enter it in his catalogue. They hide themselves at the entrance of Donna Elvira, also played by a dramatic soprano. She bewails her lover's betrayal, "Ah! chi mi dice mai," or "Ah! Who will tell me." The Don (who was in fact her betrayer, but who doesn't at first remember her) naturally wants to comfort this attractive woman. He approaches her while Leporello makes sarcastic asides on the nature of his master's type of comfort, to the orchestra's musical asides of a similar tone. But Donna Elvira recognizes him and he hastily makes his escape, leaving his servant to quiet her. Leporello does so by reading off a catalogue of Don Giovanni's conquests in one of the great comic pieces in the opera. The "Catalogue Aria" begins, "Madam, this is the catalogue of the lovelies my master has loved . . . in Italy six hundred . . . in Germany two hundred . . ." He goes on to explain that they are "women of every rank, of every size, of every age . . ." This is a classic patter song into which the librettist injected a great deal of humor and sarcasm. A patter song is an aria of many words, repeated in a very rhythmic pattern that allows for special emphasis on a subject or subjects. The idea was to cram as many words as possible into the rhythm and for the singer to sing it quickly for comic effect.

Scene Three changes to the countryside near Don Giovanni's castle. There is a celebration in honor of the impending wedding of Zerlina, a lyric soprano, and Masetto, a baritone. The happy couple enter dancing and laughing with the villagers. Don Giovanni and Leporello approach with some appreciative comments on the attractive girls. The Don introduces himself to Zerlina and Masetto and slyly suggests that Leporello lead the people, especially Masetto, to his castle for entertainment while the Don watches over the pretty Zerlina. Masetto at first refuses to leave but when Don Giovanni threatens to use his sword, Masetto is led away protesting in his short aria, "Ho capito, Signor, sì!" or "I understand, sir, yes!" Don Giovanni tells Zerlina that Masetto is beneath her. He offers to wed her in the castle and he implores her to come with him. She demurs, but in the duet "Là ci darem la mano," or "There we will join our hands together," she is gradually won over by the irresistible Don. As they are about to leave, however, Donna Elvira enters. She frantically warns Zerlina about the betrayer. The grieving Donna Anna, dressed in black, enters with Don Ottavio as Zerlina and Donna Elvira leave the stage. Since the Don had hidden his face on the dark night of the Commendatore's death, Donna Anna does not recognize the criminal. She begs him to help her find the murderer, to which he happily agrees. Returning, Donna Elvira attempts to warn them against Don Giovanni, but he explains that she is a madwoman. In the confusion Don Giovanni manages to get Donna Elvira to leave with him. (Part of the humor in this opera is that the Don is always interrupted as he is about to make a conquest, with Donna Anna here and earlier, with Zerlina, etc. The great Don Juan never gets to make a conquest during the opera at all!)

As Don Giovanni leaves, Donna Anna realizes that his was the voice of the man who attacked her and murdered her father. She tells the story of that night in dramatic accompanied recitative and then sings her aria "Or sai chi l'onore," or "Now you know." This is sung with the traditional emphasis and feeling of an opera seria aria. The aspect of an outraged lady from an opera seria sailing through an opera buffa can be very amusing. Don Ottavio pledges all his efforts in the aria "Dalla sua pace," or "Upon her peace," an aria which Mozart inserted for the tenor in the Vienna premiere who had complained that he wasn't able to sing "Il mio tesoro," the torturous second-act tenor showpiece. Mozart, who liked "to fit his music to singers as a tailor fits a suit of clothes," cordially obliged him with the lyrical "Dalla sua pace."

Don Giovanni and Leporello reenter and Leporello explains that he has entertained the villagers and kept Elvira locked out. The Don in a carefree mood sings the exuberant aria "Finch' han dal vino," the famous "Champagne Aria," boasting of the wine he will ply his guests with.

Scene Four moves to the garden outside Don Giovanni's castle that night. Masetto enters with Zerlina. To her skeptical fiancé she protests her innocence and in the aria "Batti, batti, o bel Masetto," she offers to let him beat her. Masetto begins to relent but the approach of Don Giovanni raises his suspicions again. Masetto hides to watch them. The Don sends all the guests into his castle and turns again to Zerlina. He draws her protesting into the shrubbery, right into the arms of the outraged Masetto. Never at a loss, the Don calmly explains that he and Zerlina were just going to search for him and then suavely leads them both into the castle.

Donna Anna, Donna Elvira and Don Ottavio enter the garden disguised in cloaks and masks. Their plan is to expose the guilty Don Giovanni. Leporello comes out onto the balcony to invite the "signore maschere" to the party inside, and is seconded by the bold tones of Don Giovanni himself. The three in the garden remove their masks and vow vengeance in a stirring trio before joining the revelers inside.

Scene Five is the finale of the first act. In the gorgeous ballroom of Don Giovanni's castle three orchestras are playing, each according to the social rank of the guests. One plays a minuet for the nobility, another a contredanse for the middle class and the third a German waltz, in which Leporello and Masetto join in. The brilliant blend of these three dances musically also makes a social comment. Don Giovanni has secretly whisked Zerlina away from the dancing; suddenly a scream is heard off stage. Masetto, Ottavio, Donna Anna and Donna Elvira immediately suspect the Don, who comes out holding a cringing Leporello and accuses him of bothering Zerlina. This time, however, his glib explanation is not believed and his accusers remove their masks. Recovering quickly from his shock, Don Giovanni draws his sword and escapes. The act ends in a sudden rush to follow him off the stage.

Act Two, Scene One takes place in the square outside of the house of Donna Elvira. Don Giovanni and Leporello enter arguing. Leporello is complaining about his recent treatment, but Don Giovanni tosses him a purse, which serves to satisfy him. The Don is after a new conquest, Donna Elvira's maid, and he changes cloaks with Leporello so that he can slip unnoticed into the servants' quarters. Disguised as his noble master, Leporello stands beneath Donna Elvira's balcony, when the lady herself appears. From the shadows, Don Giovanni sings a serenade and works Leporello's arms, puppetlike. The Don asks Elvira to come to him. Believing her lover has returned to her repentant, Donna Elvira rushes down to Leporello. As they embrace, the real Don leaps out like a robber and frightens them away. Left alone to woo the maidservant, the Don gleefully picks up his mandolin and sings a lovely serenade beneath her window, "Deh vieni alla finestra," or "Come to the window." Once again, however, he is interrupted, by Masetto and others who have been searching for the guilty Don Giovanni. Disguised as Leporello, the Don successfully imitates his voice and states that he, Leporello, has turned against his noble master. He helpfully suggests that the searchers go off in different directions and, when left alone with Masetto, proceeds to thrash him. Zerlina comes on to find Masetto lying sore and bruised in the street where Don Giovanni has left him; she proceeds to comfort him in her lyrical aria "Vedrai, carino," or "You will see, dear," promising him a very nice cure.

The curtain for the second scene rises on the garden of Donna Anna's palace once again. Leporello, still disguised as Don Giovanni, and Donna Elvira appear. The wily servant is becoming afraid and wants to be rid of the amorous lady, and when Donna Anna and Don Ottavio enter, he tries to escape, right into the hands of Zerlina and Masetto. Poor Leporello finds himself surrounded by those with a grudge against his master, who also think that he is Don Giovanni. The forgiving Donna Elvira pleads for mercy for the Don. Nothing is left for him to do but to remove his disguise and escape their vengeance.

Don Ottavio is now convinced that the Don is the guilty one and that he must be brought to justice. Concerned for the grieving Donna Anna, he sings the beautiful "Il mio tesoro," or "My treasure," an aria of great technical difficulty. The scene ends with Donna Elvira's sorrowful "Mi tradì," or "I am betrayed," though this aria is occasionally cut in modern performances.

Scene Three takes place in a graveyard that night. The statue of the murdered Commendatore is seen among gravestones and monuments. Leporello meets Don Giovanni, who boasts of his conquest of the servant girl who had thought he was Leporello, and when Leporello demands to know, "What if it had been my wife?" he replies, "Better yet!" As the Don laughs a deep bass voice sounding from the graves advises him that his mirth will soon be over. At first Don Giovanni thinks that someone is on the other side of the wall, but when the voice speaks again, the Don notices the statue of the Commendatore. Leporello reads the inscription and, as instructed by the irreverent Don Giovanni, sings a patter song inviting the Commendatore to dinner. To Leporello's horror, the statue nods acceptance and the curtain falls as the Don drags his servant away to the castle to prepare for the festivities.

Scene Four takes place once again in Donna Anna's palace, where Don Ottavio in recitative pleads with Donna Anna to let her love for him console her for her father's loss. Yet she

won't let him speak to her of love in the dramatic "Non mi dir," or "Do not say." This is a demanding aria with a great deal of coloratura, but again must be sung in the unyielding, unrelenting manner of an opera seria heroine.

Scene Five moves to the banquet hall of Don Giovanni's castle. Musicians are playing and women laughing beside a laden table where Don Giovanni is dining. (The musicians are playing selections from popular operas of the day. These are operas that are now forgotten, but were once more popular than Mozart's, by the composers Vicente Martín y Soler and Giuseppe Sarti. The orchestra next plays "Non più andrai" from Mozart's own *Nozze di Figaro*, a very funny "inside" joke which Leporello tries to sing through a mouthful of pheasant.) Suddenly Donna Elvira bursts in and the Don sends away the women and the musicians. She kneels before him and humbly begs him to mend his ways, but he laughs and mocks her sincerity. As he raises his glass in a mocking toast to women and good wine, she leaves him in disgust, only to scream in horror at the sight she sees at the door. Leporello goes to investigate and he too calls out in terror at the sight of the statue of the Commendatore, come to dinner. Don Giovanni himself goes to let the statue in and attempts to entertain his stone guest as the orchestra thunders forth fearful music. Leporello hides under the table. The statue now invites the Don to dinner in turn and asks for his hand on it. Ever defiant, Don Giovanni agrees and exclaims with surprise at its cold and icy feeling. It is the grip of death. The statue demands that the Don repent, but he haughtily refuses again and again. Smoke and flames engulf them both as demons summon Don Giovanni to hell. Leporello watches them vanish amid spine-tingling chords.

Moments later Donna Anna, Don Ottavio, Donna Elvira, Zerlina and Masetto enter with the police. Leporello now crawls out from under the table and relates the horrifying events. Then in a comic finale of strictly opera buffa character, Don Ottavio obtains Donna Anna's promise to marry him in a year, Elvira decides to retire to a convent and Leporello says he will find a new master. All sing of the just end to a wicked life. (Due to the opera's length this finale was omitted in the Vienna production and usually is omitted in that city to this day.)

Comedy or drama? It's a mixture of the best of both, offering great dramatic and comic opportunities for the singers. Great Don Giovannis, who are magnetic and handsome, are hard to find but can carry the most indifferent performance. The most notable of this century was Ezio Pinza, a basso, who combined voice and looks with an effectively amorous manner. One of more recent vintage was the Italian basso Cesare Siepi.

Orfeo ed Euridice

The last opera we consider here is historically one of the first, as it is the oldest dramatic opera in the popular repertory. It's really the longest-running hit in opera history. *Orfeo ed Euridice* by Christoph Willibald Gluck was premiered in its

Italian form in Vienna, October 5, 1762. The French version, *Orphée et Eurydice*, was performed in Paris on August 2, 1774. Since then, the opera has never been out of the repertory for very long. Usually presented in its Italian form, with some of the French ballet music and arias added, the opera's lead is today sung by a contralto, instead of the original castrato. The role was rearranged for contralto by no less a musician than Hector Berlioz.

This opera is the closest we have in the modern repertory to an opera seria. With all of its essential differences, *Orfeo* has many things in common with the opera seria form. It was composed for a castrato lead, its story comes from classical mythology and features a classic *deus ex machina* to help with a happy ending. But it was the reforms which Gluck and his librettist Ranieri Calzabigi initiated in this work that have helped keep the opera in the repertory; a simplicity of story as opposed to a cumbersome plot, and delineation of character and plot in terms any audience would and still do understand.

The opera's story is based on the Greek legend of the singer Orpheus and his wife Eurydice. For dramatic purposes, the legend was slightly changed, as will be explained further on.

At the start of Act One, Orfeo is mourning at the tomb of his newly dead wife, Euridice. Shepherdesses and shepherds bring flowers to her grave and join in with mourning choruses. Orfeo, son of Apollo, the god of music, and Calliope, the muse of epic poetry, laments with such effect that Amor, the god of love, comes to him and gives him permission to descend to the underworld of Pluto to seek out the shade of his lost Euridice. There is one proviso: if he wants to bring her back to earth with him, he must not look at her until he has recrossed the River Styx. Amor conveys this to Orfeo in the lovely "Gli sguardi trattieni," or "Thy looks restrain."

At the entrance to the underworld the Act Two curtain rises. The Furies guarding the gates perform a dance to impressively stormy and agitated music. They ask who dares to disturb Cerberus, the dog guarding the entrance, and attempt to frighten away the dauntless mortal. But when Orfeo sings, "Deh placatevi con me! Furie, larve, ombre sdegnose, vi renda

PLATE 11. *Louise Homer, the American contralto who sang the title role in* Orfeo *in the celebrated Toscanini-led performances at the Met. (Author's collection)*

almen pietose," "Do not threaten me! Furies, spirits, angry
shades, be moved at least to pity," his sweet voice charms these
beasts into relenting and they let him pass. As he passes into
the underworld, the Furies and spirits gradually subside with
the music.

Scene Two moves to the Elysian fields. The happy spirits of
the blessed dance to sublime pastoral music. This "Dance of
the Happy Shades" is a marvel of classic purity, with its perfect
marriage of drama and dance, expressing the essence of happiness and serenity. The music for this ballet comprises one of
the greatest passages in all of opera, one that has rarely been
equaled and never surpassed.

Orfeo sings of their happiness and the beauty of the scene.
"Che puro ciel," or "How pure the sky." The spirits bring
Euridice to her husband. He takes her hand and leads her
away, carefully averting his eyes as Amor instructed him.

Act Three takes place on a gloomy pass under great cliffs. As
Orfeo leads Euridice upward, they sing of their happiness in re-
union. But she begins to wonder why Orfeo doesn't look at
her. She asks if he no longer loves her, if she has lost her
beauty. Orfeo tells her that the gods will not allow it, but she
is insistent. At her piteous reproaches, Orfeo can stand it no
longer and turns, singing "Amata mia sposa . . ." or "Beloved
wife . . ." Euridice falls lifeless. In his great sorrow and despair
Orfeo sings his most moving lament, "Che farò senza Euridice?" or "What is left without Euridice?" and is about to
join Euridice in death when Amor again intervenes. Amor, the
deus ex machina (the age-old device by which authors change
fate through heavenly intervention), tells him not to despair,
that he has proven his constancy. The god wills Euridice to
rise again. Joyfully, Orfeo sings "Trionfi Amore," or "Triumphant Love," and, before the temple of Amor, is joined by cel-
ebrations of chorus and ballet. All sing to love, "All'amor voi
ognor," or "To love evermore," and a stately ballet of happiness and celebration is performed.

As in all of the other operas we have examined, the story
and music are perfectly wedded. For all time, Orpheus will
sing to the music of Gluck. Although the opera's happy ending

has been criticized by purists, as the original legend ends with the death of Eurydice after Orpheus looked upon her, the audiences of Gluck's time would not have stood for such unrelieved tragedy in an evening's entertainment. And how can one quarrel with the noble and glorious finale that Gluck and Calzabigi improvised, the celebration of love?

Love is the thread which runs through the six works we have examined. All feature showcase arias which are songs of love addressed by one singer to another. In *Bohème* it is "Che gelida manina"; in *Faust*, "Salut, demeure"; *Aida*, "Celeste Aida"; *Tannhäuser*, "O du mein holder Abendstern"; *Don Giovanni*, "Il mio tesoro"; and "Che farò senza Euridice" in *Orfeo ed Euridice*. While these arias differ according to the style of the work, their common intent is basically the same, and each demands the same passion and feeling in execution. We also find a love duet common to each work: "O soave fanciulla" in *Bohème*; *Faust*'s Garden Scene; the Nile Scene in *Aida*; the love duet at the beginning of Act Two of *Tannhäuser*; "Là ci darem la mano" in *Don Giovanni*; and "Vien con me, o diletta," from the third act of *Orfeo*.

But the ensemble pieces are handled quite differently by these six composers. While all the operas possess trios, quartets and larger ensembles, they are used in very different ways dramatically. *Faust*'s Garden Scene features Faust and Marguerite falling in love while Méphistophélès amorously diverts Martha. Cunning, innocence, lechery and duplicity are the characters which make up this quartet. In the scene beginning with "Addio senza rancor," Rodolfo and Mimì reconcile their differences against the bickering of Marcello and Musetta. There is similarity here in the contrast of love and struggle. But in *Aida*, Radames, Amneris and Aida sing of secret feelings of pride and love in their trio in Act One, with its undercurrent of rivalry and foreboding. Orfeo, Euridice and Amor, on the other hand, sing their trio to happiness and love without ulterior design. In *Don Giovanni*, the masked Donna Anna, Donna Elvira and Don Ottavio sing of their plans for vengeance and are joined by Masetto and Zerlina for the next ensemble, united in their accusations against the Don, who, diverting their attention to Leporello, makes his escape.

The composers also had different uses for the overture. Gluck was one of the first to use the overture as a distinct part of an opera, giving it a thematic correspondence with the rest of the work and sometimes leading it directly into the action on stage. Before Gluck the overture had been used as a prelude to the performance, to settle the audience down and simply get everyone in the mood. Mozart, Verdi and Wagner continued Gluck's thematic and dramatic use of the overture, while Gounod wrote an overture mainly to amuse the audience while it was getting seated and quiet. The overture to *Faust* is quite nice as a musical prelude. Puccini, the verist, wanted to "get on with it," and after a few bars, the opera has already started.

The element of ballet is all but left out of the dissimilar *Bohème* and *Don Giovanni*. Nineteenth-century verismo operas had no patience with, as they saw it, extraneous forms like ballet, and eighteenth-century opera buffa rarely included ballet since opera ballets tended to be used more for dramatic coloration than comedy. Ballets in Mozart's time were used almost exclusively in opera seria, and a ballet for *Don Giovanni* or any other of his nonseria operas was probably never even considered. On the other hand, Mozart included important ballets in *Idomeneo* and *La Clemenza di Tito*, which were works based on Gluck's opera seria model, a model that included very splendid ballet elements as exemplified in *Orfeo*. The ballet scenes of *Faust* and *Tannhäuser* are quite major components; the ballets in *Aida* are less important, but decorative nevertheless.

It is interesting to examine the different vocal techniques necessary to sing the six operas we have discussed. For the first, *La Bohème*, very little bravura technique is required, save sufficient breath control for sustained legato singing and enough power for the climaxes. The singing is pretty straightforward, and coloration and vocal flexibility are not often called upon.

Aida is quite similar in its requirements but it is a little more difficult to sing than *La Bohème* because of the exposed high notes for the soprano lead, while an accomplished *messa di voce* (see Glossary, Appendix IV) is required of the tenor for his demanding "Celeste Aida." This opera also calls for a steady tone and lots of lung power.

With *Tannhäuser* and *Faust*, we find a necessity for coloratura techniques, *Faust* for its French elegance and *Tannhäuser* for its exhaustive vocal demands. Marguerite needs a good trill and flexibility for the brilliant coloratura of the "Jewel Song," while the tenor must have sufficient control of his head voice to sing the lyrical "Salut, demeure." The role of Méphistophélès includes some very difficult arias which also require flexibility and a trill. In *Tannhäuser*, both the tenor and the soprano roles call for neat passage-work with a hint of coloratura.

It is the operas of Mozart and Gluck which require the most advanced techniques. Gluck's arias are relatively streamlined, compared to much of the music of the period, but again the bel canto techniques of a good trill, perfect legato and, for Orfeo, bravura singing are needed to perform *Orfeo ed Euridice* properly.

Don Giovanni must be sung exactly in rhythm, something easier said than done; and it must be properly passionate and expressive, something almost impossible for all but the most accomplished singers. Mozart wrote some very difficult arias for Donna Anna especially: "Non mi dir" and the recitatives she must sing before both of her arias require great agility, drama and strength. Appoggiaturas and coloratura are demanded of the baritone or bass who sings the Don in order for the music to make its greatest effect. And, as we know, even one of the first tenors to sing Don Ottavio found "Il mio tesoro" murderously difficult. It is a coloratura piece of the greatest complexity that has best been solved, on record at least, by the legendary John McCormack (see Appendix II—Opera on record).

The size of the orchestra varies for these six operas. *La Bohème*, *Faust* and *Aida* use the normal-size orchestra of eighty or so players, while *Tannhäuser* needs about one hundred. *Don Giovanni* and *Orfeo ed Euridice* demand an orchestra much smaller, under sixty players. For various reasons, however, these eighteenth-century works are usually given with more players in larger houses than they were written for. This may not seem an important point, but the textures of the music sound quite different with large-sized orchestras, while the singers have to struggle harder to project their voices over the orchestra pit.

Comparing the six composers' other works with the ones we have examined, we see that *La Bohème* is similar in its require- ments to Puccini's other operas, *Tosca, Madama Butterfly* and *Manon Lescaut* among them. *Aida*, though, is representative only of Verdi's late efforts. The early operas of this great master, such as *Nabucco* and *I Lombardi*, are more reflective of Donizetti and the romantic era. Verdi's earlier operas have a considerable amount of coloratura, as do many of the operas of his "middle" period, including *Rigoletto, Il Trovatore* and *La Traviata*. All demand a florid technique from the singers, in- cluding trills and rapid passage-work.

Wagner's *Tannhäuser* is a relatively early work for him. It too looks back to the romantic era in its requirement of colora- tura technique. His later operas tend to have less emphasis on vocal display, although there are trills required of Brünnhilde in the *Ring* operas, first produced as an entirety in 1876.

Mozart and Gluck are well represented by *Don Giovanni* and *Orfeo ed Euridice*. These works are typical of their other masterpieces: *Le Nozze di Figaro, Così Fan Tutte, Idomeneo* by Mozart; and *Iphigénie en Aulide* and *Alceste* by Gluck.

In turn these composers represent the best of the eras they worked in. Mozart and Gluck were the outstanding composers of the eighteenth-century classical era. *Tannhäuser* is a good representative of the German romantic era, which began with Carl Maria von Weber's *Der Freischütz* in 1821. *Aida* is in many ways the culmination of nineteenth-century Italian grand opera, as *Faust* is of French grand opera. *La Bohème* by Puccini is typical of verismo operas, although more restrained and appealing than many of this genre.

If you enjoy these operas when you see them on stage, you will no doubt feel the same way about the other works of these composers and those of their contemporaries. There is a whole world of opera out there waiting to be discovered, representing centuries of achievement and development, an exciting repertory which has been tried and tested by generations. The operas which have amused our parents, grandparents and even their grandparents have survived the fluctuations of fortune and fashion to amuse our grandchildren and their grandchildren.

Use these operas as a departure point, a guide to choosing the performances that interest you the most. There are many unusual nonrepertory operas which you may find rewarding and pleasurable. Through this informal survey of the major schools and trends of opera via six operas that represent them, understanding and enjoying the scope of lyric theater becomes easier.

CHAPTER FOUR

Front row center

Many elements combine to make an opera performance successful; singers, conductors, directors, designers, dancers and even the audience play a vital role. Because of the many elements involved, there are people in the audience who will attend a performance for different reasons. Perhaps to see the conductor, a favorite singer, a dancer, all in addition to the prevailing reason: to see a well-performed opera. Whatever the reason, the operagoer can more fully enjoy it when he or she has an idea of what is fundamentally happening on stage and in the pit and how it is all put together.

The Singer

It all starts of course with the singer. The importance of the singer to a performance would seem obvious: no singer, no performance; but, unfortunately, successful performances are not guaranteed by the mere presence of any particular singer. It takes far more, for the job of an opera singer is enormous. It's not too farfetched to say that the great ones are the rarest and most precious jewels in the performing arts. No other performer must master two completely different arts as they must. A violinist or pianist must master an instrument and the music, and an actor, the stage and his lines; the singer must do all of that and more.

To appreciate what the singer is doing and to help the operagoer understand what the singer ideally contributes to the performance, it is useful to examine some criteria as well as some historical standards, established by tradition and history, and the operagoer can then judge personally just how well the singer is accomplishing his or her task.

To many people opera begins and ends with the singer. It doesn't matter what the opera is, what the production is like, not even how the rest of the cast performs, as long as they are able to enjoy their favorite singer. Because of this, the star system has both graced and plagued opera almost from its beginnings. The virtues of the star system are considerable. One great star of course can make an evening enjoyable, even if the rest of the cast disappoints, and if the cast is full of great stars giving their all, a memorable performance may result. A manager can take advantage of a popular star in order to perform a less-well-known opera, as he can count on the star's box-office draw to bring in a receptive audience. Certainly the singers who can sell out unfamiliar or unpopular operas are the ones that are truly stars.

Great opera stars bring something special to a performance. They have grandeur and an artistry that has been developed to a very high degree, and they are able to bring out qualities in the music and drama that lesser singers can only approximate. The singers, however, are fully aware of their worth and can cause problems for managers and the public. The term "prima donna," or "first lady," has come to be synonymous with "spoiled" and "temperamental." Prime donne, both male and female, often demand that a manager stage operas solely for them and even dictate the rest of the casting. If powerful enough, they have been known to cause a relative or friend to be engaged as conductor, even with poor credentials. With non-related conductors and co-performers, they can be arrogant, even contesting with their colleagues on stage to the detriment of the performance. Contests to see who can hold high notes the longest at the end of duets and ensembles have taken place on the stages of every opera house. But despite occasional transgressions, we still admire and love our great singers, for it's chiefly through them that the glorious works of the past become alive and vibrant again.

VOCAL CRITERIA

Traditionally, it has been most important that a singer excel as a vocalist. While there have been singers of lesser vocal ability who have made it on acting ability or stage presence alone, they are uncommon and have not always been as admired as the great vocalist.

The three things that vocally make a great singer are tone, technique and diction. No singer can truly be called great without an equal measure of these three components. Some might classify size of voice in importance with the above three requirements, but as long as the technique is sound, the average voice with a well-trained method of production should be able to be heard clearly over any orchestra conducted by a competent conductor. These requirements haven't really changed throughout the history of opera. The great music historian Dr. Charles Burney (1726–1814) gave the following criteria in his classic *General History of Music,* published in 1789, a work considered the first major music encyclopedia:

> *Good singing* requires a clear, sweet, even, and flexible voice, equally free from nasal and guttural defects. It is but by the tone of voice and articulation of words that a vocal performer is superior to an instrumental. If in swelling a note the voice trembles or varies its pitch, or the intonations are false, ignorance and science are equally offended; and if a perfect shake, good taste in embellishment, and a touching expression be wanting, the singer's reputation will make no

great progress among true judges. If in rapid divisions the
passages are not executed with neatness and articulation; or
in adagios, if light and shade, pathos, and a variety of colour-
ing and expression are wanting, the singer may have merit of
certain kinds, but is still distant from perfection.

All of this is still true today, especially if the singer is essay-
ing music of Burney's time, the music of Handel, Gluck,
Mozart and, just a bit later, Rossini. It's hard to understand,
but there are well-known singers who try to sing this music
without even being able to trill. While it may not seem so important, the trill is as necessary to this music as a period is at
the end of a sentence, a fact well appreciated by instrumentalists. Can one imagine a pianist playing Beethoven's
Fourth Piano Concerto without the trills? Yet a singer may
leave them out all through a Mozart opera, though all the
singers in such an opera were expected to trill, both males and
females. Time has not changed the nature of a singer's instrument, but it has changed traditional schooling and training.

Diction, too, is important. How long would an audience sit
through a performance of a play in which they couldn't catch
any of the words? Since opera is a sung play, the words must
be clear. Burney pointed out that any singer with poor diction
is "distant from perfection," but, surprisingly, a celebrated soprano of recent years has had a very successful career despite
being almost as famous for her poor diction as for her high
notes. It is significant to note, however, that her success has
largely been before audiences that don't understand the language of the opera.

One point Burney didn't mention is style. This wasn't too
critical in his day because almost everyone sang in the same
style. Today's singers have a much more difficult time of it as
they must master a larger repertory stretching over a four-
hundred-year period. In order to present widely different operas
properly, the singer must cultivate as far as possible the style of
the given period of the music he or she is singing. Of course
we don't know exactly how those operas sounded in the period
before recordings, but we do know much about the performing

practices of the eighteenth and nineteenth centuries from contemporary accounts.

As Dr. Burney noted, the singing of rapid divisions must be done with neatness. Most singers today, however, find rapid coloratura very difficult and need a crutch to navigate it. Commonly, the crutch used is the consonant "h" in singing scales, "ha-ha-ha," a sound very like laughing. The correct way to sing rapid passages is by using the vowel "a," or "ah-ah-ah," a far more natural and attractive sound. Such singers as Joan Sutherland and Marilyn Horne execute rapid passages properly and their methods should be models for aspiring singers of florid music.

Along with all of these thorny problems, there is the question of embellishment, also as Dr. Burney mentioned. Not only is it necessary to embellish early operas, but to know just how to embellish them. Embellishments by great singers of the past have often survived through their marked scores or from letters of composers confirming their approval of such ornamentation. Because of this, singers must wear a third hat, that of an archaeologist. Since World War II there has been an increasing awareness among musical performers of music scholarship relating to past performance practices. This movement has been largely confined to instrumentalists who seek to play antique instruments, but recently singers have shown an interest as well, an encouraging development for lovers of early operas.

In performing early-nineteenth-century music, the tenor in particular is faced with a special problem. Such music was written to exploit the two registers of the tenor voice: head and chest. Chest tones are powerful notes, which are now almost exclusively used. Singers such as the popular Luciano Pavarotti and Placido Domingo sing almost all of their high notes in the chest register. But head register produces a very different sound. This is sometimes referred to as "falsetto," an unfortunate term since there is nothing "false" about it. It is a legitimate way of singing which prevailed in the early nineteenth century. In fact, the first tenor ever to sing a high C from the chest was Gilbert Duprez in 1837. Tenors famous for their head tones included Caruso's great contemporary John McCormack, as well as the famous countertenors of recent years Russell Oberlin and Alfred Deller. A popular nonoperatic singer who uses head tones with great effect is Johnny Mathis. It's this sound which composers like Bellini and Rossini expected to hear for all of the high notes written in what are known as bel canto operas. When tenors take their high C's and D's from the chest in operas like Bellini's *I Puritani,* they do so out of ignorance and poor schooling, for they are creating an effect quite different from what the composer had in mind. A love duet or rhapsodic solo becomes martial and stentorian like the opening solo of Verdi's *Otello.* Tender music becomes hard and unyielding. It can also sound very strained since the singers are putting a lot of stress on their voices. There are tenors today that understand this and consequently are admirable stylists. Nicolai Gedda, Richard Conrad and James McCracken have all performed bel canto music with distinction and discrimination.

Even operas of the late nineteenth century present stylistic problems for singers today. These include the operas of Richard Wagner and the French school of Charles Gounod, Georges Bizet, Hector Berlioz and others. It may surprise some modern operagoers that Wagner wanted his music sung and not screamed. Early recordings by legendary interpreters of Wagner's time show that, despite his innovative rhetoric, Wagner was still a nineteenth-century composer and had not entirely turned his back on bel canto. Even in the battle cry of Brünnhilde, "Ho jo to ho," Wagner wrote in trills which are almost never sung today, though they round out the music beautifully. *Tannhäuser* contains some coloratura, as we earlier noted, especially for the male leads. Outside of Bayreuth, where Wagner designed a covered orchestra pit, big voices have always been considered a necessity for his music, simply so they could be heard. Unfortunately, many a singer without a large voice has resorted to shouting to compensate for lack of size with the inevitable lack of flexibility and subtlety and frequently the premature loss of voice.

French opera of the nineteenth century demanded a singing

style which is possibly the most refined and cultivated of operatic history. This style placed a premium on fine diction and controlled delivery or legato and forbade any excesses like open-throated shouting. Elegance of phrasing and accent make this music sound quite different than when it is sung with an Italianate or bland international approach. Operas like *Faust* have suffered greatly from lack of good French stylists. This opera, once the favorite of our grandfathers, is now looked down on and called hackneyed today, but when the music is sung properly the tunes do not sound sugary, but elegant and sardonic. Unfortunately, true French style has all but disappeared today. There are many singers who are identified as "French" but who are really so only by virtue of their passports. They get by with a pasteurized international verismo style. The performance of *Faust* listed in the discography in Appendix II will demonstrate what we are missing from most performances of this popular work. This problem has finally been recognized in France and the old Music Academy is now teaching singing again. Recently there have been faint signs of a rebirth of French style, as recordings of some of the operas of Offenbach, Auber and others feature idiomatic singers of great promise like André Maievsky and Charles Burles.

As mentioned, today's prevalent international style is the last evolution of Italian opera: verismo. Most singers are trained to sing in this style and can handle this music adequately. As it is the easiest music to master, this means that many singers halt their development with verismo, settling for the laurels easily won in performing it. Although easy to master, it is, however, very hard on the voice. Maria Callas called Puccini's music "the death of singing" because so much of it demands loud volume, especially in the upper register where it is most taxing to the average singer. Most sing most naturally in the middle of their voice, having to strain to sing extended low or high notes, which are consequently more fragile. These notes are not always the singer's by birthright, but have to be painstakingly acquired. Even Caruso had to study for years to acquire his famous high notes and he was chary of wasting them. Verismo opera is much more effective when sung with restraint. Early recordings by the creators of these operas in their first performances show a much less wild approach to the music than we sometimes get today. That this restrained, controlled approach still finds favor with audiences is demonstrated by the approval shown at performances by such artists as Mirella Freni, Montserrat Caballé and Kiri Te Kanawa.

THE SINGING ACTOR

There is probably no more misunderstood side of the singer's art than that of acting requirements. As we will see in the chapter "Opera Myths and Misconceptions," there have been many distinguished opera singer actors. For the most part, however, the primary consideration has unquestionably been vocal. Now there is a much publicized demand for good-looking singers who are accomplished actors. With the increased use of television and the apparent future of videotape and video disc, this trend can only increase. The benefits are obvious. What a pleasure to see attractive young lovers instead of fat middle-aged ones! Audiences respond more to the dramatic aspects of a performance when the protagonists are physically credible. As long as the pendulum does not swing too far and discourage people with super voices who may also have super girth, this will be a positive gain. But what opera lover who has heard Pavarotti or Sutherland would prefer thinner but inferior singers?

But attractive singers do make filmed operas much more enjoyable and in the movies one overlooks inferior vocal quality more readily than in the opera house or on records. The brilliant Ingmar Bergman film of *Die Zauberflöte* used good-looking singers who seemed to have adequate ability, but listening to the recorded sound track revealed woefully inferior singing without the gloss of visual attractiveness. It was really Bergman's triumph that he made the performance seem so much better on film.

Although some opera singers have rivaled the acting abilities of nonsinging actors of any given era, it is wrong to judge them by the same standards. Due to the demands of the music and the stylized nature of opera, singers are posed with unique acting problems. Often there are very long stretches of music through which the singer will have to stand still and concentrate on singing. This is when they have to let their voices and personalities do their acting, because nothing else can be done that simply doesn't look bad. Awkward lifting and dropping of the arms in what are sometimes called "swimming gestures" have only helped to give opera acting a bad name. Of course these do not help the drama and are really ridiculous-looking, but they seem to be a hard habit to break. For singers performing in a language foreign to the audience, these long stretches are doubly frustrating since they cannot use word coloring and any joke or dramatic dialogue is usually completely missed when not underscored by the music and action. The opera singer also has to avoid being too subtle because the size of most modern opera houses makes the performers very remote from much of the audience. So singers are forced by necessity to be grand and general in their acting. The line between excess and understatement is difficult to walk.

It has been pointed out that operatic acting still resembles in many ways the acting traditions of the nineteenth century when almost all theaters were poorly lit, also discouraging subtlety; actors had to be broad in order to make an effect. The grand and imposing style of good opera actors was recognized in Hollywood when Samuel Goldwyn signed Geraldine Farrar for silent films because he felt that an opera star like Farrar would understand even more than contemporary stage stars how to be grand and large in gesture for the early primitive cinema. As a result, Farrar was one of the few singers actually to become a legitimate movie star even without the benefit of her singing.

But even if the singer is doing something highly stylized, he or she should try to appear natural. This is the advice successful singers have given to pupils for generations and it is more true today than ever, for with the increased presence of the television camera during live performances, singers will have to act for a television audience as well as for the people in the

PLATE 12. *Popular Geraldine Farrar, seen here in Cecil B. De Mille's epic film* Joan of Arc, *was thrice blessed with beauty of looks, voice and acting ability.* (Author's collection)

opera house. Thus they must be more subtle without losing any of the large effects needed to reach their in-house audiences. Although this seems hard to do, the singers appear to be coping admirably, as recent "Live from the Met" broadcasts demonstrate. The acting has been more than adequate on these telecasts and has provided genuine dramatic as well as vocal experiences for fortunate viewers.

Acting and singing in opera have to conform to some "typed" roles. A look at the specializations in opera and the many different character parts is revealing for the view it provides of the problems facing today's singers.

Opera buffa demands a unique style. The most comical roles in these operas usually go to the lower-voiced males, the basso and the baritone. True bassi buffi are highly prized commodities in any opera company, as only with them can operas like Donizetti's *Don Pasquale* and *L'Elisir d'Amore*, Rossini's *Barber of Seville* and Mozart's *Don Giovanni* be performed with success. The basso buffo is the clown of opera. He makes each syllable sound funny as he rolls it off his tongue. A special, very broad handling of the recitative and an exact comic rhythm is vital. The most distinguished buffo of our time is Fernando Corena, whose fine schooling has enabled him to sing buffo roles with distinction for many years. He carries on a noble tradition of great buffi which include the fabled Luigi Lablache and Salvatore Baccaloni. The female counterpart, and sometimes antagonist, to the basso buffo is the soubrette. By employing a buffo and a soubrette in his *La Serva Padrona*, Giovanni Battista Pergolesi set a pattern which held until the early twentieth century. The soubrette is usually a clever servant girl, a minx or even a starring comic part, such as Rosina in *The Barber of Seville*. The soubrette may be sung by a mezzo-soprano or lyric soprano, vocal distinctions which did not really even exist when most buffa operas were written. The most important ingredient in a soubrette is charm and piquancy. Like the basso buffo, a good soubrette can steal the show. For many years in Glyndebourne the soubrette, Irene Eisinger, was the favorite of the audience despite the presence of many other fine stars. Occasionally there will be a good buffo role for a tenor, such as Don Basilio in *Le Nozze di Figaro*, but such parts are much rarer, since the tenor was by this time usually cast as the romantic lead and his chief requirement in a buffa opera is elegance and an easy manner.

In total, the ideal singer should be a great vocalist, with schooling in music history and style, combined with the powers of a fine acting ability and physical attractiveness. With all of this, he or she is equipped to be a fine singer. There remains only one ingredient to be added to make a singer great: personality. It is this last ingredient which separates the great artist from the excellent one and few really have or ever have had it. This is the star quality that every manager looks for. Personality galvanizes a performance and creates the most lasting impression upon an operagoer. Unfortunately, this last qualification cannot be taught. Fans of Maria Callas remember her more for her personality than for the way she sang any given phrase; one expert who saw the legendary Lillian Nordica recalled that it was her stage presence which impressed more than anything else. Personality, although intangible, can be heard in the singing as well as seen in the acting. It is a vital force and no one who saw Maria Callas and Tito Gobbi, for example, on stage will doubt this. Another singer who built a career through her personality was Beverly Sills. The operagoer should keep this in mind when watching a singer; when the miracle of personality occurs, we can appreciate what is happening, although how it is happening remains a mystery.

The Conductor

"Nobody ever paid a nickel to see a man's back," was the opinion of a conductor's worth by Metropolitan Opera manager Maurice Grau, during the Met's great Golden Age of the 1890s. He was wrong, of course, but it is an opinion which is probably still held dear in the hearts of opera managers.

Despite the presence at the Met of many great conductors through the years such as Anton Seidl, it was Arturo Toscanini who first made the public aware that the conductor was more important to the success of an opera performance than the greatest stars, even the popular Enrico Caruso, who was the biggest attraction at the Met when Toscanini arrived. The Maestro's assertion to Caruso's co-star, Geraldine Farrar, that "There are only stars in heaven," proclaimed that he was in charge and would not allow singers to distort his performances. Although this broke the absolute rule of opera singers, it is still only the strongest and greatest conductors who are able to wield this type of authority, which is so necessary to ensure an opera's success by molding the singers into an ensemble able to deliver a unified performance.

Not only Toscanini, but other great conductors, including Bruno Walter, Gustav Mahler and Sir Thomas Beecham, felt that the opera house was where their most important work was done. It does take a very special conductor to excel in opera, as its demands are so much more diversified than those of orchestral music.

The conductor must be able to master all of the styles of the different operas he conducts and to be able to impart these styles to the singers and the orchestra. He is responsible for every aspect of the performance, not just the coordination of the singers and the orchestra through careful rehearsal and cues during the performance, but the entire tone of the work. He is really the fulcrum of the complete performance. The conductor shapes the music and the staging and has a strong influence on the action on stage. Despite explicit directions in scores, there is a wide latitude for the conductor. No one way is, of course, more correct than another, but the music should *sound* right to you, the listener. This is less simple than it seems, for the different types of opera must be approached differently. Opere buffe should sparkle and move at a fairly rapid pace; sluggishness makes them sound dull. Dramatic operas must have power and strength and a slack tempo robs them of that. Classical eighteenth-century opere serie should move with grace and nobility. These are of course very general guidelines and most opera conductors are well aware of them. Within these guidelines, however, is a great deal of room for interpretation and approach and this is where the individual temperament and personality of the conductor take over. Toscanini, Walter and Wilhelm Furtwängler all led celebrated performances of Beethoven's *Fidelio* which, while being faithful to the music, were nevertheless quite different.

As Irving Kolodin observed in his *The Metropolitan Opera*: ". . . an axiom of opera production: while a bad conductor can do more to spoil a performance than a bad singer, a good conductor can do more to ennoble it than a good singer."

It is small wonder therefore that many of today's opera superstars are the conductors. Names like Leonard Bernstein, Sir Georg Solti, Karl Böhm and Herbert von Karajan have as much box-office pull as any opera singers.

You don't have to be an expert to know if the conductor is doing his job. If you are simply enjoying the performance and the music, you can feel sure that the conductor is doing a good job. But it is illuminating to look at some fundamental things all good conductors must do to create a successful performance.

Are the singers together? It is up to the conductor through rehearsals and a steady beat to ensure that singers begin and end together and not in a ragged fashion. Is the tempo or pace even and smooth? The conductor should not alternately rush and slow down the tempo in an erratic manner. Do the singers find the tempi comfortable? If the conductor conducts too fast or too slow, the singers may sound out of breath or swallow their phrases in order to keep up. Can the singers be heard over the orchestra? With some star conductors the chief fault is an insensitivity to the problems of the singer in being heard. If you don't hear the singers, it is clearly the fault of the conductor (unless the singer is absolutely voiceless, a thing not usually found on the stage of a major opera house).

The conductor is not an accompanist as many singers may believe, but with the singers, he forms a partnership that must work both ways. The conductor has to be responsive not only to the singers, but to the rest of the company as well.

So give ample credit to the conductor when you enjoy a performance. If you are bored or indifferent to an acknowledged masterpiece, however, it is all too often the fault of the conductor. Like a general in battle the conductor has to marshal great forces, hundreds of musicians, singers, extras and even stagehands; and like the general, he is ultimately responsible for the results. It is by inspiring those forces into giving a great performance that the conductor triumphs. No one who has experienced the emotion and electric excitement of one of those incandescent nights in the theater can doubt that the one most responsible is the conductor.

The Stage Director

These days one hears as much about the stage director as one does about singers and conductors. One might say that they've become the newest stars in opera, although there are singers and conductors who will privately maintain that most stage directors do little more than stand around and let the singers have their way. Still, there is little doubt that stage directors have had a great impact on many of the productions we see around the world.

The stage director is responsible for the dramatic qualities of the stage production. He must be able to envision the work as a finished product, a dramatic whole, and help the singers, chorus and extras to carry out the total conception. Of course he has a great deal of help with many operas. Many composers, including Wagner, Puccini, Meyerbeer and others, were quite specific in what they wanted. And what they did not initially spell out in the printed score, stage book or libretto was usually clarified through their letters to conductors and regisseurs (the ancestors of stage directors). It is the clear duty of a stage director to help the singers and the rest of the company to bring the composer's conception to life.

The total effect of ensembles, timing and unity must be helped by the stage director. He has to guide the singers and chorus on and off the stage. He has to group and choreograph the chorus and extras on stage for maximum visual effect, as nothing is more boring in opera than a chorus that simply ambles onto the stage and then becomes a part of the scenery. When the score calls for it, the stage should whirl with life. The best stage directors of today accomplish this with wonderful consistency. Brilliant directors like Frank Corsaro and Tito Capobianco have had remarkable success with the chorus as well as the singers.

At some point the stage director, who is ultimately responsible for the visual effects of the production, must get together with the designer and determine the approach and designs. Of course this is made easier in the case of a few directors who perform both functions; at the very least they can then agree. Sometimes there is a danger that these powerhouse stage director/designers will sabotage the work of the composer, as in the recent Metropolitan Opera production of Wagner's *Der Fliegende Holländer*, which saw the composer's story changed to conform with the wishes of the director/designer. This is a more frequent danger in Europe than in the United States, however, where audiences do not receive productions of this sort with much patience.

But most of the time, the stage director and designer working together ensure that the unity of dramatic effect will be maximized. If the director sees the opera as a bright powerful affair, he will want the designer to design his scenery and costumes accordingly. Or if he wants a somber effect to create a moody atmosphere for tragedy, this too may gain in the collaboration.

The Designer

Basically the designer's function is like the director's, to carry out the wishes of the composer through his designs, using as a guide the instructions in the performance book and drawing on the history of past designs, examples of which are in great abundance. The good designer will be careful to set the opera in the time period in which it is supposed to take place, and make sure that the costumes conform with the period. If the libretto calls for a specific setting such as a castle or forest, the designer will make sure that there is a convincing one on stage. Things really haven't changed very much in the sense that the public still loves a richly lavish, realistic set and the most popular and durable designers have always understood this and delivered it. Current designers such as Nicola Benois, son of Diaghilev's great designer Alexandre Benois, and Franco Zeffirelli are famous for their splendidly lavish sets, which are often alone worth going to see. With one of these designers, an opera like *Aïda* is sure to be a fabulous visual spectacle. In the United States, Nathaniel Merrill and Robert O'Hearn form a brilliant director-designer team which has given the Met and other companies rewarding productions.

Their productions of the Strauss operas *Die Frau ohne Schatten* and *Der Rosenkavalier* are probably the two productions which bring the highest credit to the Metropolitan Opera. Certainly none have more fully taken advantage of the splendid resources of that institution.

It is the designers who understand color and are not afraid to use it who have the greatest success. The designer who tries to be chic or clever, who gives us bare palaces or monochromatic sets, usually falls out of fashion quickly.

The most recent phenomenon of opera design is the unit set. This is a money-saving set or unit which is turned or modified during the opera to function during all of the acts. Sometimes such a device works quite well, but often the motivation is solely money-saving at the expense of the production values. One recently publicized production of Meyerbeer's *Le Prophète* at the Met involved a unit set that was a sort of monkey bar arrangement alternately supposed to represent a wheat field and the Münster cathedral. For such a long opera, the audience developed visual fatigue from seeing the same arrangement for each act. Meyerbeer had understood this danger and his original production was famous for its lavishness and detail. Producers who ignore the imperatives of a work do so at great peril. On the other hand, the New York City Opera used an ingenious baroque-looking unit set for their production of *Julius Caesar* which remained faithful to the needs of the opera. Unit sets are neither good nor bad, they just shouldn't be the catch-all solution to every design problem.

Often downright impoverished and empty productions, even on occasion a bare stage, are defended in the media as getting into the psychological meaning of a work. The great American stage designer Robert Edmond Jones properly labeled such productions as "cheap productions masquerading as art."

One wonders why some designers do this today, when with all of the technical wonders at his disposal, the designer can accomplish more than ever before. There are production techniques which can create harmless but impressive fires, storms, and ghosts. When an institution such as the Met uses these in a production like *Die Frau ohne Schatten*, both the audience and the work are the beneficiaries.

Ballet in Opera

The most neglected element in opera is surely the dance or ballet. Of course there are many operas which don't even include ballets, including the popular Puccini and most Wagner operas, but in many operas the ballet is a very important ingredient and often a very misunderstood one. And it is not just the public which misunderstands the role of ballet in opera, but sometimes conductors, managers, and even choreographers and dancers. To understand just how far the fortunes of dance in opera have fallen, we will briefly review the glorious, sometimes checkered history of ballet in opera.

In France in the seventeenth century, the ballet took precedence over singing. These works were not even called operas, but *tragédies-lyriques*, or lyric tragedies. The *tragédie-lyrique* reached its height in works by the composers Jean-Baptiste Lully and Jean-Philippe Rameau, including *Alceste* by Lully and *Le Temple de la Gloire* and *Les Indes Galantes* by Rameau. These were given in an unbelievably lavish manner by the French Court with the royal palaces often mere backdrops to the spectacle. Central to these were the dances. Eventually the *tragédie-lyrique* gave way to conventional grand opera, but the importance of the dance in France remained so strong that not until recently could an opera be staged at the Paris Opéra without a ballet incorporated into it. Wagner wrote the famous Venusberg ballet for the staging of *Tannhäuser* at the Paris Opéra, but put it into the first act rather than the second as traditional fashion prescribed, and the late-arriving Jockey Club members rioted when they found that they had missed the ballet! Wagner had to flee for his life.

Italy and Germany too had dance in opera seria, often at the end of the opera, usually in celebration of the happy resolution of the story.

The nineteenth-century grand operas made much use of ballet and the "Ballet of the Ghostly Nuns" in *Robert le Diable* by Meyerbeer was danced by the legendary Marie Taglioni, the most famous ballerina of the nineteenth century. This work had a great influence over the growth of romanticism in the performing arts. Earlier, Auber had cast Taglioni as the nonsinging lead in his opera *La Muette de Portici* (*The Dumb Girl of Portici*).

Operas written during the last half of the nineteenth century with significant ballets include Verdi's *Otello* and *Aida,* and of course *La Gioconda* with its famous "Dance of the Hours" by Amilcare Ponchielli. In Russia, the ballet was naturally prominent and included the famous "Polovtsian Dances" in *Prince Igor* by Alexander Borodin.

Most verismo operas did not include ballet, but the American musical has made extensive use of dance, most notably in *Oklahoma!,* which featured ballets by Agnes de Mille, and *West Side Story,* which was choreographed by Jerome Robbins.

Ballet was included in all of these works for important reasons. In all they add to the grandeur and spectacular impact of the work as entertainment. In some they serve as an alternative to comic relief of dramatic pressure, as in the ballet sequence in *Otello,* which occurs as Otello has been thrown into jealous frenzy. They add necessary color and movement to the stage and relieve the possible monotony during some of the longer and more stylized operas, and, as stated earlier, they have a special use at the end of many baroque operas as a dramatic reinforcement to the happy ending. *Idomeneo* by Mozart has a particularly lovely ballet at its conclusion. Clever composers who were canny showmen often used the ballet to make striking effects. No one understood this more than Meyerbeer, who astonished Paris with his "Les Patineurs" sequence in *Le Prophète*, which used roller skaters to give the illusion of ice skating on the stage of the Paris Opéra.

In many instances, ballet is a crucial element in the development of the drama itself. One of the most striking and intensely moving instances is the "Dance of the Happy Shades" in Act II of *Orfeo ed Euridice* by Gluck. Gluck uses the ballet to show how happy and contented the ghosts of the dead are in the Elysian fields. This is one of the greatest of all opera ballets and certainly offers the lover of dance an opportunity to see a ballet performed to music far superior to much of the standard ballet fare.

When these operas were given originally, they featured the best dancers available. In the nineteenth century impresarios engaged opera troupes and ballet troupes together. La Scala, the Paris Opéra and other major opera centers were also the centers of dance and usually had famous dancing academies. Today this is no longer true. Although most major opera companies maintain ballet "wings" they are largely made up of lesser-quality dancers than ones in celebrated independent troupes like the New York City Ballet or American Ballet Theatre. While it is usual practice for the great opera companies to try to cast the best stars in singing roles, these companies rarely attempt to put great dancers in the ballet parts. Only occasionally has a luminary like Nureyev or Violette Verdy appeared in an opera ballet. And this is the dancers' great loss as well as ours. For in many cases the opera ballets are superior to the flimsy divertissements that are currently danced in ballet companies. The giants of music like Mozart, Gluck and Verdi provided much finer music than all but a few ballets in the current repertory. Attempts by the ballet companies to perform excerpted ballets from operas rob these ballets of dramatic context. We and the dancers also miss out on entertainments which could feature the best singers and dancers together. Some opera managers have been aware of this and have tried from time to time to upgrade the ballet at their companies. The Met tried to have George Balanchine and later Dame Alicia Markova improve the ballet at the house, but the sorry state of ballet at the Met today shows that they had little impact. Balanchine occasionally provides choreography for opera ballets such as the Met's *Orfeo,* but these occasional forays by great dancers and choreographers only leave us anxious for more. For it is a lot to ask even of the best to achieve very much on such a limited basis.

Choreographers who approach opera are faced with the same problems as singers, conductors and dancers. They must be aware of the style and period of the work. Dance technique has changed a great deal over two hundred years and it is not always easy for the dancers to simulate an old style. Choreographers have not always understood the requirements of a period and have made mistakes, such as having ballets like those in *Orfeo ed Euridice* or *Dido and Aeneas* feature dancing on point, a technique developed far later than the operas named were written.

Occasionally impresarios have to deal with another problem when they encounter a role which calls for both singing and dancing. The most well-known of these is the title role in *Salome* by Richard Strauss, featuring the celebrated "Dance of the Seven Veils." Usually the resolution involves a soprano executing a simplified dance, waving her veils madly. The Met tried the most unusual solution for its very first performance of *Salome,* when a dancer substituted for Olive Fremstad in the "Dance of the Seven Veils." This solution was found to be less satisfactory than the less experienced dancing of a good singer.

There is good reason for optimism, however. We are now in the midst of what is called a new Golden Age of dance. Recent television and movie exposure has done as much for dance as for opera, and what was once not the most popular of the arts is today the most popular. It was in response to this recent growth of popularity of dance that the New York City Opera featured a double bill of opera and ballet: *Dido and Aeneas* by

Henry Purcell and *Le Bourgeois Gentilhomme* by Richard
Strauss. Although the ballet, *Le Bourgeois Gentilhomme*,
starred Rudolf Nureyev and was choreographed by George
Balanchine, *Dido* was more interesting. The famous dancer
Peter Martins choreographed the extensive ballet sequences
and the American School of Ballet, which is operated by the
New York City Ballet, used some of its best pupils for them.
While not perfect historically or artistically, it was an admira-
ble and enjoyable experience which it is to be hoped will be
repeated.

Revivals in Europe of opera ballets, such as *Les Indes
Galantes* and *Le Temple de la Gloire* of Rameau, point to the
increased interest in seeing authentic eighteenth-century ballet.
The summer festival at the Drottningholm Court Theater in
Sweden provides seekers of authentic theatrical experiences
with a unique opportunity to view not often seen operas, including their ballets, performed in copies of the original costumes, frequently in original settings, with scholarly recon-
structions of the old dance techniques. Surely it is only a
matter of time before all opera companies provide these works
along with the usual verismo fare.

The recent cooperation of the New York City Opera and
the New York City Ballet, and the now permanent residency
of the American Ballet Theatre in the Metropolitan Opera
House, although not during the opera season, has given hope
that these companies will begin to pool their resources and
give the American public the pleasure of seeing their favorite
stars in both arts perform together.

The Audience

As with the opera singer, the importance of the audience
would seem simple: no audience, no performance. However, it
is not enough just to have the seats filled, because the audience
really plays a crucial if unconscious role during the performance. A knowledgeable and enthusiastic audience will spur the
performers to strive for their very best. Equally important is a

polite audience, since nothing can spoil a performance more than inconsiderate latecomers or early leavers parading up and down the aisles. Today's audience is expected to sit quietly when not applauding, and coughing and unwrapping of candy are sins which can and should be avoided. If audience members follow the golden rule, there is usually no problem. But when they don't, as is too often the case, they can certainly lessen the enjoyment of their fellow patrons.

A problem that has plagued conductors and impresarios has been applause before the end of the music. Sometimes the emotions of a thrilling performance cannot be denied, but composers have often written some of their loveliest music at the end of an aria or duet, music which many people have never heard because of applause coming right after the singer has finished. Sir Rudolf Bing tried to get Metropolitan Opera audiences not to applaud until the end of the performance without success and since then management seems to have given up asking.

Still, we have come so far in audience behavior that it's amusing to look at audience demeanor of the past. As previously mentioned, old prints show that attending the opera was quite a different affair from today, and written accounts confirm the visual evidence. Perhaps the best way to imagine an opera performance of a century or more ago is to relate it to a sporting event of today. There are striking similarities. Vendors moved among the audience hawking their wares out loud. The sounds of open conversation and the tinkling of glasses intermingled with the music from the stage. Only when something extraordinary took place on stage would something resembling respectful attention occur in the audience. It would surprise many of us to learn how recently this was the fashion at opera and theater performances. It was Richard Wagner who was chiefly responsible for the reforms which included darkening of the house for the performance. Formerly the auditorium had been brightly illuminated for the audience's comings and goings. Conductors like Toscanini and Mahler continued Wagner's fight. There are amusing drawings which show the glare of Mahler's monocle as he stared down talkers and latecomers. These men rightly wanted the performance to be heard in a quiet, attentive atmosphere. Of course an eighteenth-century operagoer or even the composer might find the atmosphere too stuffy, but few of us would want to revert to those old days.

Even today, in Italy especially, some of the old traditions hold, one of which is booing in disapproval. Americans going to such festivals as Verona's or even performances at La Scala bring home tales of Italians hurling programs and the old familiar tomato at singers they don't like. One famous story says that a sarcastic audience kept bravoing at the end of the tenor's aria. Thinking that he was making a hit, the poor man finally asked if he might continue, although he appreciated their approbation, and was answered that he could continue only after he had sung the aria properly.

That type of activity is almost unknown in America. Boos are rarely heard, although some people have speculated facetiously that they might not have to suffer through as many bad performances if they were more vocal in their disapproval. Some booing has been heard at the Metropolitan in recent years in response to some bad productions, to the distress of the management.

The problem of the claque has also given booing almost the appearance of self-defense, for management and singers have been known to hire professionals to applaud and cheer, discouraging the proper method of audience disapproval: silence. Claques are one of the more unfortunate aspects of the opera experience. They have even been known to blackmail singers with threats of booing if they are not paid off with free tickets and, occasionally, money. Ezio Pinza gives a clear account of such activity in his autobiography, *Ezio Pinza*, which describes the Met claque of his day. Management seeking any help possible will sometimes resort to hiring a claque to cheer for new opera productions or to guarantee the success of a debuting singer. Claqueurs are very sophisticated in their approach; they applaud at just the right moment with cheers and bravos to influence the audience to respond in a like manner, thinking the performance was better than they had realized. Of course, management would be better off paying for improved productions and singers, but the claque would still threaten to boo. This need not bother you at a performance, but it is interesting to be aware of the possibilities of a claque. Sometimes the claque unintentionally exposes itself when, during a cool reaction from the audience, they can be clearly heard cheering in a concentrated group from the upper reaches of the house or from standing room.

After a performance, it's fun to be able to cheer, and this is the way to do it: for all of the performers, yell "Bravi!" To applaud a single male singer, yell "Bravo!" and for a female singer, "Brava!" This is simply the plural and the masculine and feminine singular of the Italian cheer meaning "Hooray!" Some might hesitate to cheer in this way from self-consciousness perhaps, but it is the perfect way to express your approval of a glorious performance; the singers really do love and appreciate sincere demonstrations of this sort. And being able to cheer in such a way after an exhilarating performance is a nice advantage over the silent television audience. All that they can do is turn off the TV, but in the opera house you can tell the singers in the best possible way, "Thank you."

CHAPTER FIVE

Where to see an opera

Today the world is enjoying an opera boom, especially in evidence in the United States, where there have never been so many opera companies in existence. Many of these companies are worthy of notice and give wonderful performances. Some, of course, are more consistent than others and it may be useful to have an idea of how the opera you want to see will be handled by different companies. Can the opera house deal with the technical difficulties? Can they assemble a proper cast or will they produce the opera in a way that is faithful to the demands of the composer? This chapter takes a look at the major opera companies in the United States and Europe, as well as the popular music festivals around the world, and should make it possible to choose a performance which can provide optimum pleasure.

Opera in the United States (The Major Companies)

Opera in the United States is undergoing a tremendous change. Although it is still dominated by the handful of major

companies led by the Metropolitan Opera, increasing activity
on the regional scene has been impressive. The major companies in the United States form an unofficial "Big Five."
They are considered major for several reasons: the length of
their seasons, national prominence and exposure through
broadcasts, and the quality of their productions. All of the
major companies feature the top international stars as well as
top directors, conductors, designers and production values. The
American "Big Five" stack up as follows:

THE METROPOLITAN OPERA

The most important opera company in the United States is
the Metropolitan Opera House in New York City. It was
founded in 1883 in opposition to the older established Academy of Music. There were so many wealthy people in New
York unable to obtain boxes in the old Academy that the "new
guard" built the Met to accommodate themselves. It was the
performances with such legendary stars as Jean de Reszke,
Nellie Melba, Marcella Sembrich, Lilli Lehmann and Lillian
Nordica in the 1890s and Enrico Caruso, Feodor Chaliapin,
Geraldine Farrar, Emmy Destinn and Amelita Galli-Curci in
the 1900s under such conductors as Arturo Toscanini and Gustav Mahler that gave the Met an unrivaled reputation that has
held up through good and bad times since. In 1966 the Metropolitan moved to its new house in Lincoln Center, a move
which for some severed the link with its golden past.

The Met at Lincoln Center is still the major American
opera company. No other opera house in the country has so
long and varied a season, combined with an annual national
tour that features performances in Cleveland, Atlanta, Memphis, Dallas, Philadelphia, Detroit and Minneapolis. With the
traditional weekly matinee broadcasts from the house in Lincoln Center and the important and ever increasing television
exposure through the broadcasts of the "Live from the Met"
series on PBS, the Met is truly a national institution.

The new Met is unrivaled in its technical equipment. Gifted

with such resources, the Met can stage splendidly even the most difficult and complicated works. The Metropolitan is also superbly professional in such little-appreciated but vital areas as lighting, make-up (perhaps the finest in the world) and properties.

With all of these advantages, it's no wonder that the routine level of performance at the Metropolitan is one of the highest in the world. If the former high Metropolitan standard of singers has fallen off over the years, this is more indicative of the drop of the level of singing in general than of the failings of the Met in particular. Certainly it is rare today for any excellent singer not to sing eventually at the Met. With the age of jet travel it is easy to contract any singer for a performance, but hard to keep him or her for any decent length of time necessary to build the particular ensembles which used to distinguish the fine opera houses of the world. Such ensembles, or groups of singers performing together with regularity at one house, are really teams, giving stability and continuity to any performance. Once La Scala, Vienna, Paris and the Met all had singers who were particularly identified with them. Now the rosters of these houses will often be strikingly similar. The Met in recent years has been trying to mold an ensemble, but it's not an easy task, considering the unfavorable tax situation for foreign singers in this country and the decline of the dollar against world currencies.

The Met has other serious problems. In spite of its long season, its repertory is amazingly static. Ever since the early 1930s, conservatism has characterized this institution. Originally the excuse was that it was all the opera house could do to survive during the Depression. But nothing has changed during the intervening years. So, while the Met has been producing an endless round of *Aidas*, *Carmens* and *Bohèmes*, other houses have reaped distinctions with brilliant performances of *Anna Bolena* with Callas, *Julius Caesar* with Beverly Sills, *Lucrezia Borgia* with Montserrat Caballé or *Les Huguenots* with the most stellar group of singers assembled in one opera since the Second World War.

The Met, of course, is aware of this problem, but, unfortunately, their forays into unusual repertory have sometimes been marked by disaster, apparently the result of misguided and inconsistent policies. When *Les Troyens* by Hector Berlioz was presented, it was given a vulgar, garish production that obscured the opera's classical lines. On the other hand, for their first production of a Meyerbeer opera in decades, originally works of lavish spectacle, the Met chose to do a "cheapie" production, stripping the work to the barest possible outlines. They had placed their reliance on the star performer to provide the fireworks needed, but she became ill, sang poorly and left the inadequate production to stand on its own, to resounding failure. When the management presented *Esclarmonde*, many critics questioned the policy which produced perhaps the poorest and most insignificant opera of a lesser composer like Jules Massenet, when some of the great masterworks of Mozart, Gluck, Luigi Cherubini and other giants have never been seen on the Metropolitan's stage.

But the most unfortunate of all the Met's problems is the opera house at Lincoln Center. Backstage it is splendidly equipped, but the part that the audience sees is like a nightmare of kitsch from Miami Beach or Las Vegas. The critics rejoiced when the Kennedy Center in Washington, D.C., was built and declared that at last there existed an uglier opera house than the Metropolitan; but this writer disagrees. Kennedy Center seems a model of dignity and restraint compared to the tawdry finery of the Met. Sadly, all of this is a strong hindrance to the enjoyment of opera at Lincoln Center. For example, the proscenium of a theater is vitally important because it serves as a frame for the stage, and an opera house almost never gets dark enough to obscure it. The Met's proscenium is, to put it charitably, a twentieth-century opera horror, and the effect of such a proscenium on a nineteenth-century opera is that of a cheap, gilded plastic frame on a Rembrandt painting. At least one director, Nathaniel Merrill, was aware enough of this problem to try and solve it for his production of Verdi's *Luisa Miller* by creating a "proscenium within a proscenium." He had rows of old-fashioned stage boxes and a quaint arch over the stage. A charming solution, but a poor substitute for the genuine article.

One can only wonder that New Yorkers allowed the historic old Metropolitan Opera House to be destroyed with hardly a protest, but became almost hysterical at the possible loss of Radio City Music Hall.

THE NEW YORK CITY OPERA

A few steps away, almost literally in the shadow of the Metropolitan Opera, is the second most important opera company in America, the New York City Opera.

The New York City Opera was founded in 1944. Established as a lower-priced alternative to the Met, the New York City Opera gave its first performance under director László Halász with a production of *Tosca* featuring the famed Dusolina Giannini.

Being so near the Met, the City Opera has an obvious identity crisis. But at its most innovative and exciting, its productions have a vitality and spirit rarely approached by the Met. Although the New York City Opera has featured some legitimate stars, it was by forging a true ensemble of young singers coached by innovative directors that the City Opera has treated New York to superb lyric theater.

And the New York City Opera has been daring and creative. With the production of Handel's *Julius Caesar*, not only was the great fame of Beverly Sills established, but New York saw what George Bernard Shaw considered the greatest opera ever written. To this date the Met has never done an opera by Handel or Claudio Monteverdi, another composer in the City Opera repertory. Even if the New York City Opera's production of Mozart's *Idomeneo* was burdened by an atrociously inappropriate stage design, at least it introduced to New York what is considered Mozart's grandest opera in its first New York stage performance.

Lately, there have been disturbing signs of change. It has almost appeared as if the City Opera was challenging the powerful Metropolitan, in direct competition with productions of such Met staples as *Turandot, Rigoletto, Tosca* and *Lucia di Lammermoor.* When the New York City Opera was housed in the City Center and was presenting such standard operas at bargain prices, there was no problem. But the great expense of operating at Lincoln Center has forced the prices up beyond any pretense of a bargain. The seats are full-priced, and by presenting works one can find across the plaza at the Metropolitan, City Opera is only inviting comparisons which do neither house any service. At the same time, the City Opera has been presenting the Gilbert and Sullivan light operas and Franz Lehár's operetta *The Merry Widow,* works done much better by companies that specialize in them, such as the Light Opera of Manhattan.

Optimism is high, however, as NYCO's greatest luminary, Beverly Sills, has assumed direction of the company. She will still have to contend with the New York City Opera's greatest problem: the New York State Theater. If the Metropolitan has an acoustic problem with some of its orchestra seats, the New York State Theater has not one seat with good sound. Singers simply hate to sing there as the sound is hollow and flat, echoes and does not carry. As is common knowledge, the State Theater was built primarily for dance, and the considerations which make it an ideal dance theater for the New York City Ballet have made it very poor for opera. Eventually, the City Opera may have to move, but no such move is in sight and one must resign oneself to the poor sound in order to see operas one may never see anywhere else.

While unquestionably still second to the Met, the New York City Opera is gaining national exposure through PBS "Live from Lincoln Center" broadcasts and as a resident opera company in Los Angeles for four weeks annually.

Also deserving of consideration by New Yorkers is the excellent little theater in the Juilliard School, in which the cream of the most prestigious music school in the United States now presents operas in a style which would not discredit its Lincoln Center neighbors. Productions of operas like Ernest Bloch's *Macbeth* and the American premiere of Richard Strauss's

Capriccio show that close attention must be paid their endeavors.

Outside of New York, the most important opera companies in the United States are the San Francisco Opera Association and the Chicago Lyric Opera. As they are tied for third place in importance, we will give preference here to the seniority of the San Francisco Opera.

THE SAN FRANCISCO OPERA

The San Francisco Opera is the second oldest opera company now operating in the United States. It was founded by Gaetano Merola in 1923. Under its recent director, Kurt Herbert Adler, the San Francisco Opera Association has gained an enviable reputation for excellence. It has a shorter season than the New York City Opera and the Metropolitan, about fifty-five performances a season in the War Memorial Opera House, and has not had much national exposure. But recent PBS national television and radio broadcasts of its performances indicate it will play a larger role in the national scene in the future.

If the San Francisco Opera presents only ten operas a year, they make every one count. Exciting repertory combined with imaginative casting have given the San Francisco Opera its fine reputation. With a longer season the company should maintain this progress.

A recent development among opera companies is the sharing of productions, and the San Francisco Opera has done some notable collaboration with another major, non-New York company, the Chicago Lyric Opera.

THE CHICAGO LYRIC OPERA

The Chicago Lyric Opera, founded in 1954, is very similar in attitude and quality to the San Francisco Opera Association.

94

The Lyric presents about seven or eight operas during its autumn seasons and it too makes them count. In 1978, the whole opera world watched when the Lyric gave the world premiere of the Penderecki opera *Paradise Lost*. Despite the verdict that it was another vapid modern opera, it was an interesting and praiseworthy attempt by a major opera company to keep grand opera a living art. It was especially commendable when one imagines the pressure upon all directors to produce popular favorites only, like *Bohème*, *Traviata* and *Carmen*. Yet when the Lyric does produce these staples, they are usually done outstandingly. In fact, the Metropolitan borrowed Chicago's production of *La Bohème* in 1977.

THE HOUSTON GRAND OPERA

The Houston Grand Opera is the newest of America's major opera companies. And while it is the youngest, founded in 1955, it is easily the most innovative and exciting. Under the inspired direction of its general manager, David Gockley, the Houston Grand Opera gives six operas a year both in the original language and in English. Although this is a relatively small season, its influence has been enormous, especially in the Southwest, where the HGO operates the Texas Opera Theater, a touring company, and gives in Houston a series of free opera performances, not in concert form, but fully staged. This is where the now famous Broadway production of *Treemonisha* by Scott Joplin originated. Through this and the tours and Broadway runs of Gershwin's *Porgy and Bess*, which also played successfully in Paris, and *Hello, Dolly!*, they are seriously rivaling the Metropolitan Opera as a national institution. To their credit, the Houston Grand Opera has realized that Broadway musicals are American opera and has staged them, in sharp contrast to other major companies, which only produce such works when composed by a European composer like Kurt Weill.

PLATE 13. *The Houston Grand Opera's hit production of Scott Joplin's* Treemonisha, *starring Carmen Balthrop. (Photo courtesy Houston Grand Opera)*

Regional Opera in America

The Houston Grand Opera's approach to opera will surely be a model for other major companies and the burgeoning regional opera troupes in America. As opera continues to increase in popularity, more and more companies are springing up across the country. For the most part these regional companies are of very high quality. Within certain technical limitations their productions do not differ too greatly from those of major companies and they often feature top international stars. These companies are doing great service for opera. They are reaching new audiences with enlightened policies like opera in English and innovative staging and repertory.

A company which verges on being a major one is the San

PLATE 14. *The San Diego Opera production of Ambroise Thomas's* Hamlet *featured Sherrill Milnes and Ashley Putnam. (Photo courtesy San Diego Opera)*

Diego Opera. Under the vital direction of Tito Capobianco, the San Diego Opera, founded in 1964, is making itself felt on the national scene. This is an ambitious company which has given such productions as the rarely staged *Hamlet* of Ambroise Thomas and the premiere of Gian Carlo Menotti's *La Loca*. The company stages six operas a year and has inaugurated the world's first festival devoted to Giuseppe Verdi (see American Opera Festivals).

One of the oldest regional companies gaining national prominence is the Greater Miami Opera Association. Founded in 1941 by Arturo di Filippi, the company is now the largest and most influential opera company in the South and is bringing

PLATE 15. *Miami presented* Falstaff *with the beautiful sets of designer Nicola Benois. (Photo courtesy the Miami Opera Guild)*

great excitement to south Florida. The Miami Opera has always featured the finest singers, but it has also been distinguished for presenting unusual repertory. Miami's emphasis on the too often neglected French repertory brought it recognition from the French Government. Often Miami's lavish staging is the envy of the opera world. Recent productions of Verdi's three Shakespearean operas featured a unified staging, marvelously designed by the talented Nicola Benois. Miami gives four to five operas a year, both in the original language and in a "Family" English series.

The Opera Society of Boston, established in 1958, has commanded its share of headlines. Led by the flamboyant Sarah

Caldwell, its founder, the company has presented the American premieres of Berlioz's *Les Troyens* and *Benvenuto Cellini*. It presents about fifteen performances a year.

Founded in 1963, the Seattle Opera is another very good company. Its emphasis is on the traditional repertory, presented with a good mixture of young "comers" and established stars. Most important of all is its summer festival devoted to Wagner (see American Opera Festivals), which has gained international attention.

The Dallas Civic Opera, founded in 1957 by Lawrence Kelly, gives fine performances of mostly standard operas. They made a notable departure, however, during the 1950s when they presented Maria Callas in such operas as Donizetti's *Anna Bolena* and Cherubini's *Medea*. Recently Dallas again made news with their controversial staging of Vivaldi's great *Orlando Furioso*, the American premiere of a masterpiece.

A very special regional opera theater is the Goodspeed Opera House in East Haddam, Connecticut. This fabulous Victorian opera house was built in 1876 and was restored as a historic landmark in 1963, when it became a living theater once again. The Goodspeed Opera House is devoted mainly to the American musical and has become a unique institution through revivals of such historic musicals as *Whoopee!* and *Babes in Arms*. It also features new works and first produced *Man of La Mancha*, *Shenandoah* and *Annie*. In an idyllic setting on the Connecticut River, music and theater lovers are able to enjoy a bouquet of revivals and new creations, an enviable accomplishment on the part of the Goodspeed company.

The number of regional theaters grows daily, and to examine all of them is not the purpose of this chapter. Virtually every city in the United States of any size now gives opera performances of some kind. In addition to those already mentioned, we might include the Cincinnati Opera, which gives six operas annually in the historic and beautiful Music Hall, built in 1873; the New Orleans Opera, which gives a few operas a year with major singers (alas, a pittance compared to the former glory of this city, in which the major opera company in America once gave performances in the French Opera House);

PLATE 16. *The Goodspeed Opera House, an enchanting Victorian theater on the Connecticut River. (Photo courtesy Goodspeed Opera House)*

the Baltimore Civic Opera, which was a pet project of Rosa
Ponselle's; the Cleveland Opera; and the Milwaukee Opera.
Hawaii, Newark, Memphis and Pittsburgh also have troupes.
No doubt some of these will join the ranks of the major
leagues someday.

A scene of activity which commands our increasing attention
although it still has a long way to go is Washington, D.C.
Through the completion of the John F. Kennedy Center for
the Performing Arts and the activity the Center has generated,
there have been some productions worthy of the status of our
nation's capital. The Metropolitan Opera will give performances in the Center, moving from the outdoor arena at Wolf
Trap, and visiting opera companies such as La Scala and the
Vienna State Opera are featured occasionally. During the summer there exists a promising chamber opera series, but, ideally,
Washington must begin to present its own opera company in a
significant way.

American Opera Festivals

With the rapid growth of opera in the United States, it
shouldn't be surprising that a country which is relatively new
to summer festivals now has several of international prominence. Once summer for the affluent opera lover meant a trip
to the prestigious European festivals in Salzburg or Bayreuth,
but most of us are now able to "see (opera in) America first!"

The Santa Fe Opera Festival
Santa Fe, New Mexico

New Mexico is hardly the place one might associate with
opera, but the Santa Fe Opera Festival has been making quite
a name for itself. In twenty-six performances during the summer, it presents unusual and daring works. It has given world
premieres by such composers as Villa-Lobos and Berio, along
with the American premieres of such diverse works as Alban
Berg's *Lulu* in the unfinished version and more recently the
three-act version, and Cavalli's *L'Egisto*. Their productions and

stage direction have combined with this interesting repertory to make even New Yorkers aware of opera in New Mexico.

The Central City Opera Festival
Central City, Colorado

The oldest opera festival in the United States, founded in 1932, is the Central City Summer Festival. Quaint old Central City, the center of much of the gold prospecting in this country from 1859 to 1893, is now a gold mine for opera lovers. The beautiful restored Opera House built in 1878 is where fine performances, usually in English (this was the first festival to advocate opera in our native language), have included such premieres as *The Ballad of Baby Doe* by Douglas Moore. A recent production was the revival of an opera presented to the Central City miners in 1877, the English ballad opera of Michael William Balfe, *The Bohemian Girl*. In Central City the bar of the Teller House, the beautiful old hotel, is the place to go for informal recitals.

Spoleto Festival, U.S.A.
Charleston, South Carolina

Perhaps a more likely place for a festival is Charleston, South Carolina. Charleston is one of the oldest cities in America, with a gracious beauty that has even survived both the Civil War and the twentieth century. It is full of beautiful revolutionary houses and gardens. In fact, the first performance of opera in the United States was given in Charleston, possibly as early as 1702. As Charleston was also the first city to have a symphony orchestra, one can only wonder why it took so long for a major festival to arrive here.

It was Gian Carlo Menotti, when he decided to establish his Spoleto Festival in the United States, who finally brought major opera back to this great old city and inaugurated in 1977 what may well prove to be a bigger attraction than his original Spoleto Festival in Italy. The beginning has been most promising, and such famous stars as Magda Olivero and the great ballerina Carla Fracci have been featured.

PLATES 17 AND 18. *The Seattle Opera's Pacific Northwest Festival gives Wagner's Ring in traditional, realistic costumes and sets. (Photos courtesy Seattle Opera)*

Pacific Northwest Wagner Festival
Seattle, Washington

A festival of enormous importance to Wagnerians is the Pacific Northwest Wagner Festival in Seattle. Here one may see sumptuously staged, as it was meant to be, the *Ring* of Richard Wagner both in German and in English. Presented through the Seattle Opera, the summer performances of Wagner's *Ring* were the inspired idea of Glynn Ross and were inaugurated in 1975. For the present, this festival is the best place in the world to see Wagner, and its *Ring* puts the foolish production at Bayreuth to shame. Seattle has had the courage to present these operas as Wagner wanted them to be done. Here can be seen glorious sets and costumes which bring the dramas richly to life. One only hopes that Seattle will eventually expand this festival to include all of the Wagner operas. As of now, the festival draws its patrons from all over the world and, as it is on the West Coast, it has a particular attraction for visitors from Japan and the Far East.

San Diego Opera Verdi Festival
San Diego, California

For years many people including Arturo Toscanini dreamed of a major festival like Bayreuth devoted to the operas of Giuseppe Verdi. It has been established at last, not in Italy as one would have thought, but in San Diego, California. This festival is a new one, founded in 1978 by Tito Capobianco, who has said that "It is our aim to produce the entire body of Verdi's operatic work over the next ten years, and to expand our programming to include a format for new and experimental as well as traditional ways of producing the composer's works." He has carried through so far with performances of *La Traviata, I Lombardi, Aida* and the *Requiem,* and future plans include *Il Trovatore* with the rarely performed French ending. Combined with the natural attractions of San Diego, this festival seems sure to be a winner.

Canada is another scene of growing opera activity. Of interest is the Festival Ottawa, which will make a trip to Canada as richly rewarding for opera as for the natural beauties of Canada. Back in the United States, there are festivals which, while not primarily opera festivals, nonetheless have significant activity. These include the Aspen Festival in Aspen, Colorado, and the Mostly Mozart Festival at Lincoln Center in New York City, as well as some of the smaller-scale festivals such as the Cincinnati Summer Opera Festival and the Lake George Opera Festival in Glens Falls, New York.

When planning an operatic vacation or trip, remember that the festivals and major opera companies are very popular and that tickets are in great demand. It is a good idea to secure tickets well in advance and to pin down lodging accommodations, which can be scarce at popular festivals and in big cities.

Where to Write for Tickets and Information: U.S. Opera Houses and Festivals

The Metropolitan Opera
Lincoln Center Plaza
Lincoln Center
New York, NY 10023
Tip: Avoid the orchestra
  seats, where the sound can
  be poor
Best Seats: Dress Circle

The Metropolitan Opera
  National Tour in:
CLEVELAND: write to
Northern Ohio Opera
  Association
1400 West Tenth Street
Cleveland, OH 44113

The Metropolitan Opera
  National Tour in:
BOSTON: write to
The Met in Boston
Suite 1004
31 St. James Avenue
Boston, MA 02116

The Metropolitan Opera
  National Tour in:
ATLANTA: write to
Atlanta Music Festival
  Association, Inc.
P.O. Box 12181
Atlanta, GA 30355

The Metropolitan Opera
  National Tour in:
MEMPHIS: write to
Arts Appreciation Foundation
P.O. Box 82400
Memphis State University
  Box Office
Memphis, TN 38152

The Metropolitan Opera
  National Tour in:
DALLAS: write to
Dallas Grand Opera
  Association
13601 Preston Road
Suite 212 West
Dallas, TX 75240

The Metropolitan Opera
  National Tour in:
WASHINGTON, D.C.:
  write to
Opera House
John F. Kennedy Center for
  the Performing Arts
Washington, DC 20566

The Metropolitan Opera
  National Tour in:
MINNEAPOLIS: write to
Metropolitan Opera in the
  Upper Midwest
105 Northrop Auditorium
84 Church Street, S.E.
Minneapolis, MN 55455

The Metropolitan Opera
  National Tour in:
DETROIT: write to
Detroit Grand Opera
  Association
Ford Auditorium
20 East Jefferson Avenue
Detroit, MI 48226

The Metropolitan Opera
  National Tour in:
PHILADELPHIA: write to
Robin Hood Dell Concerts,
  Inc.
1617 John F. Kennedy
  Boulevard
Philadelphia, PA 19103

New York City Opera
Lincoln Center Plaza
Lincoln Center
New York, NY 10023
Tip: The NYCO operates in
  two seasons, alternating
  with the ballet—be certain
  of dates
Best Seats: All acoustically
  bad, but side view seats in
  the second and third rings
  offer good value

*The San Francisco
   Opera Association*
Mrs. Margaret Norton
San Francisco Opera
   Association
War Memorial Opera House
San Francisco, CA 94102
Tip: Avoid seats under the
   balcony
Best Seats: All except for
   above

Chicago Lyric Opera
20 North Wacker Drive
Chicago, IL 60611
Tip: Be sure to visit
   Chicago's older opera
   house, the Chicago
   Auditorium, designed by
   Louis Sullivan
Best Seats: All fine

Houston Grand Opera
Attn: The Subscription Office
P.O. Box 200075
Houston, TX 77216
Tip: The Houston Opera's
   Student Performances are
   excellent
Best Seats: All good

*San Diego Opera and Verdi
   Festival*
P.O. Box 988
San Diego, CA 92112
Tip: The festival includes
   films, classes, workshops
   and performances of
   Verdi's nonoperatic music
Best Seats: Orchestra

*Greater Miami Opera
   Association*
1200 Coral Way
Miami, FL 33145
Tip: The finest restaurant in
   Miami is Joe's Stone Crab
   in Miami Beach. Go early
Best Seats: Try for the front
   balcony in Dade County
   Auditorium. Avoid the
   acoustically dead Theatre
   for the Performing Arts in
   Miami Beach

Goodspeed Opera House
East Haddam, CT 06423
Tip: Stay in a quaint old
   New England inn nearby
Best Seats: All wonderful

Santa Fe Opera
P.O. Box 2408
Santa Fe, NM 07501
Tip: Short season, June 30 to
   August 25
Best Seats: All fine

*Seattle Opera and Pacific
  Northwest Wagner Festival*
P.O. Box 9248
Seattle, WA 98109
Tip: Book far in advance for
  this two-week festival
Best Seats: All good

Spoleto Festival, U.S.A.
P.O. Box 704
Charleston, SC 29402
Tip: Book for the small
  events in the historic
  theaters
Best Seats: Varies from
  theater to theater

Central City Opera Festival
Central City Opera House
  Association
University Building
910 16th Street
Suite 636
Denver, CO 80202

Tip: Book early for lodging in
  the Chain O' Mines or the
  Teller House
Best Seats: All fine in this
  opera house which seats
  eight hundred

Festival Ottawa
National Arts Centre
Ottawa, Canada
Centre National des Arts
Box 1534 Station "B"
Ottawa, Ontario
Canada K1P 5W1
Tip: Train travel in Canada
  is a special delight
Best Seats: All adequate

*Washington D.C. (see
  Metropolitan Opera
  National Tour)*
Tip: Try to catch some of the
  international companies
  which make up for the lack
  of local activity

Opera in Europe and Abroad

With the exception of the Metropolitan in New York, all of
the world's major opera houses which constitute an unofficial
global "big five" are in England and the rest of Europe. These
are the Paris Opéra, the Vienna State Opera, Covent Garden
and La Scala. Seeing an opera in these houses can be a thrilling experience, as there is special pleasure in seeing an opera
produced in the proper surroundings, sometimes even in the
house an opera originally premiered in. In these houses it is
possible to look back on a gracious time when opera was the

PLATE 19. *Milan's Teatro alla Scala as shown in an early nine-teenth-century print. (Author's collection)*

number-one entertainment. In this atmosphere a special magic is added to the performance. No need for a "proscenium within a proscenium" in these old auditoriums. Unfortunately, the productions are not always worthy of the surroundings.

Teatro alla Scala
Milan, Italy

The most fabled of these opera houses is Milan's Teatro alla Scala, built in 1778. A few of the operas which were intro-duced to the world in this historic theater are Bellini's *Norma*, Verdi's *Otello* and Puccini's *Madama Butterfly*. Although there have not been any new operas of such greatness pre-sented here lately, La Scala is still the foremost Italian opera house in the world, with sumptuous productions that are usu-

PLATE 20. *The Grand Staircase of the Paris Opéra. (Photo courtesy French Government Tourist Office)*

ally faithful to the composer's intentions. More often than not, the singers at La Scala are in their youthful prime and the level of conducting is very high. It is considered the world's most perfect opera house for its beauty and acoustic quality.

Paris Opéra
Paris, France

The Paris Opéra is another legendary house. French opera always existed on an elevated plane, and this grandest of Belle Époque temples of art was consecrated to that ideal. Walk into the foyer and you see statues of such composers as Rameau and Lully, the fathers of French opera, who almost seem to be guarding the grand tradition. Even the official name is imposing: la Grande Académie de Musique. Nor does the building disappoint. From the ornate exterior to the grand staircase inside, it is almost as if you were walking onto the ultimate opera set. But sit in a plush seat in the splendid auditorium and look up to view the magnificent ceiling, and surprise! Instead of the chandelier and beaux arts paintings you naturally expect to see, you encounter a huge mural by Marc Chagall. You may wonder how the painting got past the statues out front, and indeed at the thinking which crowned a Belle Époque jewel with an ultramodernist work. This may be taken as a forewarning, because the productions have not preserved the French tradition either. Not only are the singers the same one sees all over the world, a far cry from the once elite group of French singers formerly associated with the house, but one has to go around to the rear entrance to the wonderful opera museum in order to find the scores of Rameau, Lully, Grétry, Spontini, Cherubini and Halévy which used to make up the repertory. The Paris Opéra has become an "international" house abandoning its heritage. If it does occasionally produce a French opera, it is usually a disservice to the composer, as with its latest production of *Faust*, set in an absurd "crystal palace" contrary to the story and stage instructions.

The Paris Opéra was once famed for its ballet, which was equal in importance to the opera company. Indeed, no opera was allowed to be presented there without a ballet. Today the Paris Opéra ballet is only the merest shadow of what it was.

<h3 style="text-align:center">Vienna State Opera
Vienna, Austria</h3>

The Vienna State Opera is a beautiful opera house. It is a cream and gilt confection, worthy of the Hapsburg empire it crowned in the days when it was called the Vienna Court Opera. Now the Vienna State Opera, it is warmly recommended for several reasons. It is the most traditional of the German-language houses, and you are less likely to find a preposterous production here than, say, in Munich or Berlin. More importantly, although the Vienna Philharmonic is not the greatest orchestra in the world (there are several in the United States of superior quality), it is definitely the greatest opera orchestra, which is one of its functions under the name

PLATE 21. *The superb cream and gilt auditorium of the Vienna State Opera. (Photo courtesy Austrian National Tourist Office)*

of the Vienna State Opera Orchestra. To hear an opera played by this fine orchestra is a revelation, making one wish more opera houses would link up with neighboring concert orchestras.

Covent Garden
London, England

London's major opera house, Covent Garden, is marvelous. Interestingly, it is the only one of the major opera houses to preserve a semblance of the nineteenth-century tradition of giving great importance to the ballet. No wonder; with the famous Royal Ballet on hand, could it be otherwise? They alternate with the opera troupe and sometimes join it for performances.

The English have always been noted for their reserve, and this is reflected in the demeanor of the Covent Garden audience. One normally senses the pleasure of the rest of the audi-

PLATES 22 AND 23. *Both the interior (plate 22) and the exterior (plate 23) of London's Covent Garden opera house exude the glamour of bygone Edwardian days. (Photos courtesy British Tourist Authority)*

ence through applause and other signs of approval during the performance, conduct which is often absent in Covent Garden. But at the end of an act comes warm and enthusiastic applause, and the British, who are the most loyal audiences in the world, release all of the emotion so politely stored up during the performance.

The loyalty of the British toward favorite singers is admirable, but the visitor to Covent Garden may hear a performer of markedly inferior quality being well applauded. This loyalty to their singers, especially British ones, has sometimes built artificial reputations that don't hold up when these singers appear on stages in other countries. To avoid such singers at Covent Garden, one must choose a cast as carefully as the opera.

About the house itself there are no reservations; Covent Garden is the most elegant opera house in the world. The lines are smooth and the sound rich. One can at times almost believe that there will be another famous "Melba Night," when royalty, glittering in diamonds, thronged the house to see the favorite diva of Edwardian times.

There are of course many other opera houses of distinction in Europe. The historic Théâtre de la Monnaie in Brussels is a wonderful theater, and although the performances are not likely to be distinguished these days, they are given with a rare enthusiasm. Moreover, it's a joy to attend an opera in such lovely surroundings.

The Munich and Berlin operas give musically superior performances in fine auditoriums, but too often the avant-garde quality of their productions is so distracting that it can all but ruin an opera lover's pleasure.

Other fine institutions to consider include the Rome Opera, the English National Opera, the beautiful and historic Teatro San Carlo in Naples and the noble Teatro la Fenice in Venice, which saw the premieres of Verdi's classics *Rigoletto* and *La Traviata.* Also very important is the Bohemian National Opera of Prague, a great opera center that has to its credit the world premiere of Mozart's *Don Giovanni.* The world-famous Bolshoi Opera in Moscow recently made an acclaimed visit to New York. In truth, almost all of the beautiful, historic opera houses in Europe are worthy of a visit, if only for the attractions of the buildings themselves. Often, even in the most obscure of them, one can have an enchanting musical experience. One of the most memorable opera performances this writer can remember is one by the semiprofessional Vienna Folk Opera of Giovanni Paisiello's *Barber of Seville* in the Schönbrunn Palace Theater, a lovely Baroque jewel which brought the audience and singers into an unusual intimacy very appropriate for the old, classic work.

On other continents, too, opera flourishes. In South America there are some truly magnificent opera houses with proud traditions. The Teatro Colón in Buenos Aires, Argentina, is a splendid French Renaissance-style theater that has always drawn first-rank stars, including Caruso, Feodor Chaliapin, Giuseppe Anselmi and Francesco Tamagno, and has presented important world premieres such as Manuel de Falla's *Atlántida*. The house, built in 1908, is worth a visit for its beauty alone. A stupendous theater is the Teatro Amazones in Manaus, Brazil. Opened in 1896, it was a product of the Brazilian rubber boom when money poured in to make it one of the most ornate opera houses in the world. Once, great stars traveled the better part of a month up the Amazon at the promise of large fees. Never loath to accept a large fee, even the imperious Adelina Patti made the arduous trip. Many other fine houses are to be found in South America, which, true to its European heritage, has never lost its appetite for opera.

Australia is famous for having given the world many legendary singers, including Dame Nellie Melba and Marjorie Lawrence. It's also famous for the strangest opera house in the world, the modernistic Sydney Opera House. Among some of its more peculiar features are no wings backstage, making side entrances rather difficult, and questionable acoustics. Its famous but decidedly odd silhouette is indisputably different. A trip to Australia should include a visit to this institution, which presents decent performances with famous stars.

PLATE 24. *The Australian curiosity, the Sydney Opera House.*
(Photo courtesy Australian Tourist Commission)

European Opera Festivals

Most of the European opera houses close during the hot
summer months and are replaced by the music festivals so popular with tourists and music lovers alike. For many Americans
this is the preferred way to see opera in Europe, and the festivals can certainly be an exciting and glamorous experience.

The most prestigious festivals are the Bayreuth and Salzburg
affairs. Each deserves to be discussed at length, as they may be
the first places you will wish to visit.

Bayreuth Festival
Bayreuth, Germany

There is a special irony about the Bayreuth Festival today. It
was founded by Richard Wagner in 1876 as the one place
where his wishes and instructions would always be carried out
to the letter. No composer was ever more sure of what he
wanted in the production of his works, or left more detailed instructions about it. He wrote his own libretti and was very in-

volved in the staging of his operas and the designs for the scenery. The irony is that there is no institution in the world today which as completely ignores these instructions and traditions as the Bayreuth Festival. Perhaps more importantly, it has influenced most opera houses to do the same.

The further irony is that it is Wagner's own grandchildren, Wieland and now Wolfgang, who are responsible for the famous staging "revolution" of as bare a stage as possible. Actually this great philosophy, which supposedly allows the true psychology of the dramas to triumph over mere stage props, arose out of dire financial necessity. When Bayreuth was allowed to reopen after World War II, there were two problems. One was the stigma of Nazism and the other a lack of funds. So, citing their philosophy as a purging of the productions of German nationalism, the grandchildren economized. No doubt Wagner hasn't stopped spinning in his grave. Around the world lately a reaction has begun to set in. After so many years of praise for the minimal sets, here and there traditional productions have emerged to great encouragement from critics, who are perhaps weary of looking at next to nothing on stage. The Met production of *Tannhäuser* was a "revelation" to those who had grown up with the Wieland Wagner tradition. Now even Wolfgang has turned away from the bare stage and recently produced a fairly traditional *Parsifal*. But the current *Ring* cycle at the festival is one of the great disgraces in the history of opera. From the premiere it has been greeted with derision and boos and controversy. So unless you plan to see *Parsifal*, it is better perhaps just to take a quick tour of the festival house and museums, and only attend performances there if you want to experience in person a sad chapter in opera history.

Salzburg Festival
Salzburg, Austria

The Salzburg Festival is situated in one of the loveliest towns in Europe, and as it's Mozart's birthplace, a festival devoted to his operas is a fitting tribute. The Salzburg Festival's great performances of Mozart operas began with the ones organized by the legendary soprano Lilli Lehmann in the early 1900s. They were distinguished in the 1930s by the leadership of Bruno Walter and the participation of Arturo Toscanini. At that same time, however, the questionable practice of presenting non-Mozart operas at the festival was begun.

Mozart did not like his native city. He resented its provincialism and the ill-treatment he received there. It is unlikely that he would be any more pleased with Salzburg today during festival time, for the Salzburg Festival is the most commercial in the world. When Geraldine Farrar, a singer in the early Lilli Lehmann performances, revisited Salzburg in the 1930s she was shocked at the commercialization even then. If she could see it today, she might look back on the 1930s with fondness. It is a festival invaded by the "beautiful people," and it's ironic to see them dressed in their finery watching, in apparent ignorance of its moral, the *Everyman* play that is an old Salzburg tradition. This is the famous Max Reinhardt production of the old drama which tells of the rich man who must die like the poor man, despite his wealth and power. Tickets for the Salzburg Festival itself are expensive and often run into hundreds of dollars for one seat. It is a questionable investment, because one can see the same performances in Vienna at much lower prices and in a better atmosphere, since the theaters at Salzburg leave something to be desired. The hideous Grosses Festspielhaus actually has an iron curtain—hardly in the spirit of Mozart. One of the other theaters is the old riding school, which does have a certain charm. But Salzburg is loveliest when there is no festival and one can quietly visit Mozart's birthplace and a few other sights, then return to Vienna by a long, beautiful drive along the Danube to attend the Vienna State Opera in the evening.

Glyndebourne Festival
Glyndebourne, England

Another Mozart festival is the Glyndebourne Festival in England. Founded by an enlightened millionaire named John Christie, it takes place in a beautiful theater built on the grounds of his estate. The first performances in 1934, led by

Fritz Busch, were so famous that they were chiefly responsible for the renewed, worldwide popularity of Mozart's operas. A famous series of recordings made of the first performances is striking evidence of the excellence of early Glyndebourne.

Today, the singers are not as good as they used to be at Glyndebourne. It was never the festival's policy to hire star singers, but in the 1930s they managed to hire unknowns destined to become stars, like Ina Souez, Willi Domgraf-Fassbänder and Salvatore Baccaloni, and later a young Birgit Nilsson and Luciano Pavarotti. The singers today are young and attractive, though, and occasionally there is still a vocal find among them. What is more important, however, is that they usually form an excellent ensemble.

Non-Mozart operas are now given as well, but the spirit of the enterprise has never been lost and the productions are, on the whole, both innovative and faithful.

Edinburgh Festival
Edinburgh, Scotland

The July festival in Edinburgh, Scotland, was the brainchild of Rudolf Bing in 1947, who had been associated with Glyndebourne and who wanted to found a similar festival. Although it does not possess a comparable opera house, the performances are of a very high quality and the city of Edinburgh is absolutely marvelous to visit. Even in typically poor weather, there is a romance still very much alive in the city of Sir Walter Scott. And if there are any "dour Scots" in Scotland, you won't find them in Edinburgh.

Festival Aix-en-Provence
Aix, France

Another lovely place for a festival is the South of France, and the Festival Aix-en-Provence is a fine one. The open-air performances given in the Archbishop's Palace often consist of rarely seen Baroque and early classical operas, and are occasionally produced in a manner reminiscent of the true French tradition. In any case, Provence is such lovely country that it

would take a miserable performance to spoil things, a most unlikely occurrence.

Verona Festival
Verona, Italy

The festival in the ancient Roman theater at Verona will satisfy the seeker of opera spectacle. The acoustics of this theater, which can hold many thousands of people, make it almost intimate and one observer noted that "you can even hear the audience eating their salami sandwiches." The audience is usually very unrestrained and, if displeased, will throw food and boo loudly. The operas are staged on an unusually grand scale with celebrated singers.

Drottningholm Festival
Drottningholm, Sweden

A very special festival, as anyone who saw Ingmar Bergman's film of Mozart's *The Magic Flute* will agree, is the Drottningholm Festival (the film was made in Drottningholm). Here in a theater built in 1766 one can truly imagine one is in an earlier age. Rare Baroque and early classical operas and ballets are given with original scenery and replicas of original costumes. Quaint and fascinating original machinery for creating magical illusions is used and the orchestra even wears powdered wigs. To complete the illusion, the audience sits on wooden benches in the auditorium, just as they would have in the eighteenth century.

There are many other fine festivals. Most of the large European cities run some sort of opera festival in the summer, such as that in Vienna and the famous Spoleto Festival in Spoleto, Italy, run by Gian Carlo Menotti. All will make a trip to Europe memorable for the opera lover.

In going to festivals, especially the popular ones, it is imperative to have all reservations and tickets secured well in advance. Frankly, it would be wise to give serious consideration to a good travel agent, who can be your best source of good tickets and can recommend those special hotels or even ancient castles which can make your stay so much more enjoyable.

Where to Write for Tickets and Information
European Opera Houses and Festivals

Teatro alla Scala
Milano
Italy
Tip: Visit the La Scala
   Museum, the finest opera
   museum in the world
Best Seats: All

Théâtre National de l'Opéra
   (Paris Opéra)
8, Rue Scribe
Paris, 9e
France
Tip: Be sure to visit the opera
   museum in the rear of the
   opera house
Best Seats: All

Vienna State Opera
Staatsoper am Ring
Opernring 2
Wien I
Austria
Tip: Have the original
  famous Sacher torte at the
  Hotel Sacher Café behind
  the Opera
Best Seats: All, but avoid
  boxes

*Covent Garden Opera
  Company*
Royal Opera House
Covent Garden
London, W.C.2.
England
Tip: Eat nearby so that you
  can walk to the opera, as
  finding a taxi can be
  impossible
Best Seats: All

Bayreuth Festival
P.O. Box 2-72
Bayreuth
West Germany
Tip: Visit Wahnfried as well,
  Wagner's home, now open
  to the public
Best Seats: All

Salzburg Festival
Hofstallgasse 1
Salzburg
Austria

Tip: Be sure to make early
  reservations for an
  after-theater supper in a
  quaint restaurant
Best Seats: All satisfactory

*Glyndebourne Festival Opera
  Ltd.*
23 Baker Street
London, W.1.
England
Tip: Be sure to bring a picnic
  basket
Best Seats: All

*Edinburgh International
  Festival*
29/30 St. James Street
London, S.W.1.
England
Tip: Stay in a romantic
  Scottish castle nearby and
  avoid the crowds
Best Seats: Varies from
  theater to theater

Festival of Aix-en-Provence
Société du Casino Municipal
  d'Aix Thermal
3, Rue Frédéric Mistral
Aix-en-Provence
France
Tip: Be sure to visit the
  Roman colosseum in Nîmes
Best Seats: Varies from
  theater to theater

Verona Festival
Ente Autonomo Spettacoli
    Lirici
Via Gaetano Patuzzi, 9
Verona
Italy
Tip: Take a sandwich
Best Seats: All

Drottningholm Festival
Stockholm Festival
Festival Office
Konserthuset
Stockholm C.
Sweden
Tip: Take Swedish currency
    traveler's checks
Best Seats: All wonderful

CHAPTER SIX

Opera's buried treasures

One of the more interesting, and sometimes the most frustrating, aspects of opera is that there is a surprisingly large number of works that are no longer performed. Many of these were once in the standard repertory of the world's major houses and were given hundreds of performances, but for one reason or another they have since fallen out of favor. While today's standard repertory remains your best guide and yardstick to the operas most sure to please, you, the veteran operagoer, may tire of seeing the same works from season to season and may want to seek out new and unheard operas. Well, there is a veritable gold mine of them, many of them undeniable masterpieces that rest in undeserved obscurity.

But this is where we get to the frustrating aspect; unfortunately, one cannot really experience an opera by reading the score or libretto. It must be seen or at least heard on records to be appreciated as it deserves. Except for a few enlightened opera companies like the Houston, Santa Fe, Central City and, occasionally, the New York City operas, the large houses tend to ignore these works, partly from disinterest and partly due to the financial risk involved in staging them.

Fortunately there are some enterprising companies devoted

PLATES 26 AND 27. *The Houston Grand Opera has explored a wide-ranging repertory, including productions of Handel's* Rinaldo *with Marilyn Horne (plate 26) and Richard Strauss's* Arabella *with Kiri Te Kanawa (standing) and Ashley Putnam (plate 27). (Photos courtesy Houston Grand Opera)*

to performance of the untapped repertory of the operatic archive, and there is great activity on the part of certain record companies along the same lines. For example, the complete operas of Joseph Haydn are being recorded for the first time, as well as Verdi's, many of which are rarely if ever staged. Operas by Meyerbeer, Daniel-François Auber, Giovanni Paisiello, André Grétry, Jean-Philippe Rameau, Jean-Baptiste Lully, Handel, Claudio Monteverdi, Pier Francesco Cavalli and Georg Philipp Telemann are all available on the labels of such companies as Columbia, EMI, London, RCA, Philips, DGG and others, as listed in the Schwann catalogue. Even more intriguing are the works of Saverio Mercadante, Giovanni Pacini, Niccolò Piccinni (Gluck's great rival), Luigi Cherubini, Ermanno Wolf-Ferrari and Gasparo Spontini, among others, which are available on private labels, such as MRF.

The companies that produce such operas and sometimes stage them perform a great service for opera lovers. Two major ones are the Opera Orchestra of New York, which is led and conducted by Eve Queler, and Opera Rara of London. The Opera Orchestra of New York, which evolved from the old American Opera Society, is the major organization in the United States devoted to performance of rare and seldom performed operas. In its brief history, it has performed many obscure operas of Donizetti, Massenet, Bellini, Rossini and Wagner, all to the pleasure of one of the most knowledgeable and loyal audiences in New York. The operas are performed in concert, that is without scenery or costumes, nor are they acted out. So, while these performances are little more than live recordings, they are avidly patronized by grateful fans. The Opera Orchestra of New York presents their repertory with major international stars, such as Nicolai Gedda, Marilyn Horne and Montserrat Caballé, whose debut with the old American Opera Society launched her American career. The Opera Orchestra's season consists of concert performances of three operas a year. For information and subscriptions contact:

The Opera Orchestra of New York
10 East 53rd Street
New York, NY 10022

London's Opera Rara gives a few staged productions in addition to concert performances. A production at the Camden Festival of Donizetti's *Torquato Tasso* in 1974 was staged with great success. This company does not rely on big-name stars, but has found and developed singers some of whom have become stars, such as Yvonne Kenny and Janet Price. They seem to concentrate on the obscure bel canto operas of Bellini, Donizetti, Mercadante and the Ricci brothers, whose *Crispino e la Comare*, once a great favorite of Adelina Patti's, is a true delight. Opera Rara's productions are done with great scholarship and they have even founded an opera recording subsidiary. Information may be obtained by writing:

Opera Rara
8 Haverstock Street
London, N.1.
England

Other companies that perform mainly concert versions of rare operas include the New York-based Friends of French Opera, and the Sacred Music Society of New York, whose concert performance of *Il Crociato in Egitto* by Meyerbeer in Carnegie Hall in 1979 was received with great interest.

These groups and record companies help to fill a tremendous gap, for otherwise the total picture of opera cannot be approached. Yet today the operas we are exposed to represent only the tip of the iceberg. The standard international repertory and the relative handful of operas that have been recorded are only a beginning to opera appreciation.

Perhaps the most neglected repertory of all is French opera. In the early nineteenth century, the most popular composer of opera in New Orleans and, ipso facto, the United States, was Nicolas Dalayrac, whose name doesn't appear anywhere in the Schwann catalogue, or nearly anyplace else, for that matter. French opera is, ironically, most neglected in France, where only the activity of Radio France and sporadic, halfhearted efforts by the Opéra-Comique, a shadow of the former great institution, preserve any of the national lyric treasures. The quality of the neglected works is high. They include *Joseph* by Étienne Méhul, which Richard Wagner declared "a magnificent work, which transported me to a higher world." Today, all we know of this opera is the superb aria "Champs paternels," recorded by John McCormack over fifty years ago. There is *La Vestale* by Gasparo Spontini, known only through recordings by Rosa Ponselle and Maria Callas of the famous arias (in Italian translation) "Tu che invoco" and "O nume tutelar"; but the entire opera deserves a better fate. *La Dame Blanche* by Adrien Boieldieu has been recorded and revived, but an opera whose popularity made Bizet so jealous warrants wider exposure. Americans are almost unaware of these operas as well as great ones by Gluck, Rameau and Lully. And lovers of *Fidelio* may be interested in the opera Beethoven purposely imitated, *Les Deux Journées* by Cherubini. Beethoven thought so highly of this opera that he kept a copy of its score by his bedside. Haydn declared Cherubini the greatest composer in the world, but the Metropolitan Opera, among others, does not seem to be aware that Cherubini ever existed. The only opera by Cherubini which has had any exposure is *Medea*, made famous by Maria Callas in Dallas and elsewhere, and by a concert performance in New York with the fine singer Eileen Farrell.

While the French repertory is most neglected, there are many great German and Italian operas that have received less attention than is their due. Rossini is just beginning to be appreciated as the composer of other works than *The Barber of Seville*. Donizetti wrote many operas as fine as the perennial favorites *Lucia di Lammermoor* and *Don Pasquale* which are now being performed for the first time in many years. Two contemporaries of Rossini and Donizetti were Mercadante and Pacini, but other than a few sporadic performances and MRF recordings of their work, the two masters are forgotten today. Yet Pacini was a powerful rival of Bellini, while Verdi was effectively influenced by the works of Mercadante. The Italian composer who gave Gluck such tough competition in Paris, Niccolò Piccinni, is represented by only one entry in the MRF catalogue.

A composer whose works greatly influenced Wagner, and from whom he borrowed music for *Lohengrin*, is Heinrich Marschner. His *Hans Heiling* would be a sure favorite today.

The operas of Louis Spohr, Otto Nicolai and Albert Lortzing are almost unknown outside of Germany, except for a few recordings.

All of these works and so many more are worth reviving. In the interests of broadened music horizons, more and more of these buried treasures ought to be unearthed in the future. In the meantime, we can only fantasize about the opera we most want to see. Aside from Méhul's *Joseph*, this writer would most love to see *Una Cosa Rara* by Martín y Soler, an opera that knocked Mozart's *Figaro* off the boards in Vienna. It is heard today only in the brief segment quoted by Mozart in the last scene of *Don Giovanni*. And based on the evidence of the MRF recording, *Il Campiello* by Wolf-Ferrari could be inexpensively but delightfully mounted by any size opera company. This work was written in 1936 and, though modern, is full of melody, brilliantly set to a story by Carlo Goldoni.

One way to approach less-well-known operas is to start with the works which have the same name or story as more famous ones. Recordings of Paisiello's *Barber of Seville* reveal an opera not inferior to Rossini's more famous version, nor is Rossini's *Otello* put to shame by Verdi's more dramatic one. Other operas that have been recorded and revived because of the association with a familiar repertory opera are *Leonora* by Ferdinando Paër, based on the same story as Beethoven's *Fidelio*, and *Manon Lescaut* by Daniel-François Auber, a subject that both Puccini and Massenet treated with success. There is a wealth of interesting operas which deserve examination in this way. No doubt despite the overwhelming popularity of *La Bohème* by Puccini, Leoncavallo's *Bohème* will someday have its day in the sun.

People eventually get tired of too much of a good thing, whatever it may be, and nothing proves immune to this movement. When audiences tire of the favorites that are presented regularly, there are many, many more operas out there just waiting for a rebirth.

CHAPTER SEVEN

Opera on television and in movies

Today we are entering a new era in home entertainment. The fledgling videotape and videodisc industries foreshadow a time when the opera recording will be a visual as well as an audio one. Through the increased use of cable TV and the recent public television broadcasts of live performances of opera, operas can be introduced to millions of new viewers.

Live broadcasts of opera performances are a great opportunity for people who have not had a chance to attend an opera to see one with some of the immediacy of the theater. The excitement of a live performance with the uncertainty and tension it entails cannot be duplicated in a studio performance or taped replay.

The live broadcasts of the Metropolitan Opera and the New York City Opera, as well as national broadcasts of the San Francisco and other opera companies, including presentations from Covent Garden and the Vienna State Opera, are giving ever more exposure and popularity to opera. TV also provides one answer to the foreign-language dilemma through the use of subtitles. While some may find these subtitles distracting, management struggling for opera education for years calls their use the greatest breakthrough in opera history. Something like having your cake and eating it too, they say. Of course, this is not an entirely satisfactory solution, because translations don't allow you to understand vocal coloring or individual emphasis on words, but it is a great help to the audience and a positive benefit of the medium of TV.

The future for live opera on TV seems almost unlimited. On the "tube" smaller companies can become nationally visible. It can give financial windfalls to struggling companies and will certainly build larger audiences in the nation's houses.

Yet even the best televised opera is no substitute for the real thing. Not only is the sound inferior, but you are at the mercy of the cameraman. Close-ups of singers can be unflattering and fragile theatrical illusions are often lost, while stylized acting techniques, effective in the theater, can look comical. Even more seriously, opera can lose its grandeur on the small screen. But on the whole live broadcasts on television are a promising development which encourage people to go to the theater for the genuine experience of opera at its best.

Movies of opera, on the other hand, somehow retain opera's grandeur, the large screen accurately conveying the grand scale. And opera has had a place in the cinema from the beginning of films; even the silent era saw notable operatic films, including appearances by Mary Garden, Enrico Caruso and, most successfully, Geraldine Farrar.

The era of the "talkies" gave rise to a great deal of activity in Hollywood and in Europe on the part of opera singers. Perhaps wrongheadedly, Hollywood tried to work singers into movies primarily in dramas or comedies that featured snatches of their singing. It was in Europe that complete operas were filmed. These include outstanding films of *Louise* with Grace Moore, *Don Quixote* with Feodor Chaliapin and *The Bartered Bride* with Jarmila Novotná.

Commercially, operas have had mixed success in the movies, but the ones that are the most successful are the ones which preserve the theatricality of the work. The movies that tone

PLATE 28. *Opera on film has come a long way since the 1918* My Cousin *with Enrico Caruso.* (*Author's collection*)

down or completely negate this quality are bound to be disasters. A film by Jean-Pierre Ponnelle of *Le Nozze di Figaro* was photographed in artistically dismal interiors and featured closed-mouthed singers "thinking" their arias. This was in striking contrast to what is perhaps the most outstanding opera movie ever made: *The Magic Flute*, directed by Ingmar Bergman. This enchanting film constantly reminds us that we are witnessing a staged performance in an opera house, by showing us reactions of the audience and some charming backstage vignettes. The charm of the staged opera survived its translation to the big screen, augmented by only a few cinematic tricks. The film was made for Swedish television, but the lack of heavy-handed meddling with the story and the virtue of absolute integrity to the subject stand as a shining example to producers. The NBC Opera Theater, which gave us outstanding films of Menotti's *Amahl and the Night Visitors* and Gershwin's *Porgy and Bess* with Leontyne Price, were notable early televised experiments in the United States. Given the expense of opera to produce, however, live performances will no doubt dominate television in the future.

As noted, the new technical achievements in the video industry foreshadow even more startling changes. The possibilities of the hologram, which would actually present multidimensional images, are only in the birth stages, but the impact could be enormous. Imagine any size theater in the house with seemingly live performances.

Still it must be emphasized that as with records of opera, television and the movies can only be a supplemental or educational aid to opera appreciation and should never take the place of a live performance in the theater. The magic of the shared experience in the theater cannot be duplicated on the screen. The warmth and the intimacy of seeing opera in the opera house should always be your aim. As illuminating as it may be to witness a televised version of an opera, you will be only better prepared for the ultimate pleasure of grand opera in the theater.

CHAPTER EIGHT

Opera oddities

Despite the fact that singing an emotion is a natural expression, basically opera itself is an artificial and stylized entertainment. Moreover, it has accumulated lots of peculiar fashions and traditions over the years. Some of these have been detrimental to its image, but most simply are products of the art form's long and colorful history. At worst, these oddities are pretty amusing.

One of the more notable of the unusual facets of opera is the practice of women singing roles as men. Known as "pants" roles, these include: Cherubino in *Le Nozze di Figaro*, Siebel in *Faust*, Hänsel in *Hänsel und Gretel* and Stephano in *Roméo et Juliette*. The reasons for this are many. One is that composers wanted to take advantage of the soprano or mezzo-soprano range in the music, whether feeling that it would most properly express the role, or that it was necessary for contrast in ensembles. Having Cherubino sung by a soprano or mezzo-soprano means that this role approximates the sound of an adolescent boy so that any girlishness of the interpreter is quite appropriate. There is also the image of purity or innocence that a female can project. Of course the erotic situations which can result are not unappreciated by most of the audience. In *Der Rosenkavalier*, the Marschallin waking up in bed with Octavian, a young man played by a woman, has extra implications. In *Le Nozze di Figaro*, there is considerable erotic irony when Susanna undresses Cherubino and redresses him as a girl (which he really is). This brilliant double entendre has amused through the centuries.

While these roles were composed specifically for women to play, there are roles which were written for men with soprano voices, the castrati, and which are now perforce sung by women. The era of the castrati, aside from the gruesome physical mutilation of adolescent boys both willingly and unwillingly, represents one of the most absurd periods in opera history from a dramatic point of view. Vocally it was a period of unexcelled virtuosity, judging from the difficulty of the music written for the castrati. Legends of their greatness abound; the fabled Farinelli who later became Prime Minister of Spain was credited with curing the Spanish King's madness through his singing. But for artificiality, nothing has approached the eccentricity of having these castrated men, who bore almost as much physical resemblance to women as to men, portray Caesar, Alexander, Titus and other legendary ancient heroes. Fashion of the period demanded that they sing decked out in plumage, jewels and satin. In the name of artistic temperament opera singers have costumed themselves in some rather peculiar ways through the years, but what could equal this description by Jacopo Ferretti: "I recall having seen at the Theater Argentina, Julius Caesar falling stabbed by the foot of Pompey's statue, wearing elegant ox-tongue shoes with blood-red heels and paste buckles, silk stockings with flowers embroidered in color up the sides, olive-green knee-breeches with emerald fastenings . . ." It was even said that the great Pacchiarotti insisted upon returning the bows made to him by the audience. However, it is important to remember that the splendor of these productions went hand in hand with their artificiality to make up in total effect an exotic and lavish en-

H. Adlard Sc.

PLATE 29. *The most legendary singer in opera history was the eighteenth-century castrato Farinelli.* (Author's collection)

tertainment of vanished brilliance. The audiences of that time regularly suspended disbelief and accepted the artifices and gratuitous embellishments which were a part of the fashion in music of the time. To the people of the eighteenth century, it was as acceptable as today we find Rembrandt's setting of biblical subjects in his contemporary Amsterdam. The modern listener might well wonder at an agility and virtuosity of vocal technique that equal the demands of the Baroque masterpieces of such composers as Handel, Gluck and Vivaldi. Left as we are with the legacy of music written for castrati, those anachronistic male roles must be sung today by women. And so we find women portraying Caesar, Orfeo or Alexander when these operas are staged. Modern audiences are as willing as an eighteenth-century one to suspend belief in order to hear certain masterpieces and easily accept women singing male roles as valid theatrical experiences.

Another curiosity which demands suspended belief is something that might be called the "inconvenient aria" or an aria which totally interrupts dramatic action. Ideally the aria should enhance the drama, as in the case of Orfeo's lament over his dead wife, or Rodolfo's song to Mimì telling her of his growing love for her. Yet Puccini made the dramatic error of inserting Tosca's fine aria "Vissi d'arte" in the middle of what is in reality an attempted rape. For as the villainous Scarpia lunges at her, Tosca suddenly stops to reflect on the difficulty of living for art and love alone, leaving Scarpia politely standing by. This freezes the action of an otherwise flawlessly constructed act. Elsewhere interminable death scenes with lots of music and vigorous singing by dying people can be and often are ridiculous. At the end of *Werther*, the hero, though he has committed suicide, finds enough strength to sing two duets and a farewell before dying. By contrast, Edgardo in *Lucia di Lammermoor* dispatches himself more quickly, after singing only one aria. Operatic death scenes need not be ridiculous, as witness Mimì's in *Bohème*, or in *Traviata*, where the dying Violetta momentarily regains her strength and, like the flame which brightens before it's extinguished, sings giddily until abruptly and finally choked off.

In addition to the many eccentricities written into the drama and the music, there exist certain oddities which have been established by the singers themselves. Singers who pride themselves on their high notes sometimes cause problems for conductors by holding high notes longer than is wise or musically correct. They may engage in contests with fellow singers to see who can outlast the other at the end of a duet or in an ensemble. This can be fun for their fans, but is a disservice to the composer. Toscanini forbade such practices and, at one rehearsal, cut off Lauritz Melchior during one of his famous high notes, held too long. The same singer can be heard in a live broadcast from the Met, when he was not singing under Toscanini, holding his high notes for unbelievable lengths of time, often in competition with his co-star, Lotte Lehmann. Maria Callas once infuritated Mario Del Monaco, her Radames, during a performance of *Aida* in Mexico City by taking a high E at the climax of the Triumphal Scene, literally drowning out all of the other singers. It was spectacular, but the scene backstage afterward must have been equally so. On the other hand, a baritone once held the value for his note in their duet longer than deemed necessary by Maria Callas, whereupon she demanded his dismissal from the Met, and got it, too.

Vanity has also led singers to odd costuming. Pictures can be seen of a corseted Aida, as sung by Adelina Patti. The cloaks by Adrian of Hollywood which swathed Helen Traubel and Lauritz Melchior in *Tristan und Isolde* could have tented armies. Proud of her golden hair, Grace Moore wore it without change for her performance of "bruna," or brown-haired, Tosca. Mattia Battistini, who refused Verdi's request to sing *Falstaff*, finding the fat knight beneath his dignity, always wore white gloves as the half-savage Amonasro in *Aida*. Franco Corelli as the poor Bohemian Rodolfo would wear fabulous patent leather shoes that blindingly reflected the stage lights. But as in the age of the castrati, these lapses may be indulged, for we expect opera to be grander than reality and our opera stars to look regal in almost any circumstances.

Perhaps the oddest situation of all is the one in which audiences attend performances of opera in a language different from their own. There is simply no question that much of the effectiveness of opera is missed when the audience cannot follow the words. Those who insist that it is best to retain the original because the music sounds best as set to the language it was composed for have carried the point in the United States. But often the reason for lack of translation is the conviction of many that the libretti are so inferior or hackneyed that translation is hardly worth the trouble. Of course this generalization

is totally wrong. The libretti by such eminent poets and drama-
tists as Pietro Metastasio, Lorenzo da Ponte, Arrigo Boito,
Hugo von Hofmannsthal and Maurice Maeterlinck are of great
merit for their literary quality alone. And the supposition that
opera sounds so much better in the original language loses
much of its persuasiveness when there are so many singers who
are not native to the language of the opera they are singing.
While some performers are undoubtedly fine linguists, many
more are really not all that proficient in languages and often
have poor diction and a worse accent when singing in a foreign
language. The most easily refuted argument against opera in
English is that, since most opera singers are foreign anyway,
they don't sound well singing in English. But with so many
American singers in theaters all over the globe, many at the
Met, New York City Opera and other American institutions,
there exists the probability of performances in good English.

The anti-English attitude was properly summed up by the
great British critic Edward J. Dent, who wrote in his book
Opera that "there are still some connoisseurs who maintain
that it is sacrilege to perform any opera except in the language
in which it was originally written. Sometimes this attitude is
due merely to exclusiveness, to pride in their own exaggerated
critical sense for vocal technique or in their intimate knowledge of foreign languages. Still the position is a logical one and
if consistently maintained would forbid all translation of literary works."

Many American opera companies do present opera in English. Houston, the New York City Opera, Central City, Santa
Fe, Miami and others regularly give performances in English,
as either the primary or the alternate performances, thus
affording American audiences a chance to enjoy repertory
works on all levels. Some, like the Met, however, largely resist,
perhaps in deference to the snobbery which scorns anything
not original. In Europe performances in native languages have
long been a common practice and the English National Opera
in England, the Vienna Volksoper and very often the major international companies present translated works.

Given good translations there is very little vocally lost in an

English translation. A performance from San Francisco of *The Magic Flute* in 1975 was broadcast in English. The singers, including the excellent New Zealand soprano Kiri Te Kanawa, enunciated perfectly and with frequent laughter and delighted applause the audience was audibly charmed with the comprehensible comedy. Even in the radio broadcast one was able to follow almost every word of the opera clearly. This is in direct contrast to performances in the original German in American houses, where the audience sits quietly through all but the broadly pantomimed comedy and where the only noise is that of scattered laughter from German-speaking patrons.

The fact that opera has succeeded so universally, even in foreign languages, demonstrates the inherent musical strength and natural dramatic quality of the art form. The sensual and emotional qualities of music in dramatic situations have often been enough to carry the idea, generally if not literally. Yet people who have loved and enjoyed opera in foreign languages, perhaps with the aid of a printed translation, will find through a good performance in their native language new levels of appreciation and comprehension.

Another oddity of opera is the anachronistic mystique of the opera box. Opera boxes are still in demand at the box office today, despite the fact that many who purchase seats in them have found themselves unable to see anything on stage. Due to crowded conditions and the angled view, opera box patrons usually have a poorer view than the standees in the orchestra, at ten times the price. The heyday of the opera box goes back to the eighteenth, nineteenth and early twentieth centuries when many went to the opera not to see, but to be seen. Society dressed itself in its best clothes and costliest jewels to sit in the front of opera boxes and provide a source of wonder and interest to the audience and fellow boxholders. This gave rise to the famous "Diamond Horseshoe" of the old Metropolitan Opera House, the horseshoe of boxes in which the cream of New York high society displayed itself. True to tradition the boxes remain today, even in some newly constructed theaters, but they are usually the poorest seats in the house. Only in the front seats of the center boxes are the views really good. The box is primarily a social institution and while it can be fun to procure an entire one for yourself and friends, you had better be good friends since not all of you will have good seats. Today the interest in opera is primarily as an artistic experience and not as a social function. No doubt most opera houses built in the future will eschew the opera box altogether.

Novice operagoers may be surprised to see the prompter's box on stage, usually in the center of the front edge. It may be shocking to learn that many singers rely on the prompter for their lines during a performance. Often this "feeding" of lines is audible to the audience, both in the house and to those listening during broadcasts. Old and new broadcasts from the Met feature a prompter who can be quite loud at times. Although singers ideally should know all of their roles by heart, it's understandable that with all of the roles in a singer's repertory in so many different languages he or she wants the comfort of the prompter. Even if the cast has thoroughly rehearsed an opera and knows all the words, should one participant become ill or indisposed the replacement might need quite a bit of prompting.

There are some very amusing stories on this subject. Once when Lawrence Tibbett had to cover as Valentin in *Faust* at the old Met people hid behind scenery in every possible place to prompt him. The occasional audibility of the prompter is of course preferable to a singer totally flubbing lines or even whole passages. Certain smart directors and singers have used the prompter's box in inventive ways; Ezio Pinza as Figaro would sing "Non più andrai," with one foot on the box, and a recent Papageno in *The Magic Flute* at the Met sat on the prompter's box, to the amusement of the audience.

Once a common occurrence, the encore, or the practice of stopping a performance to repeat an aria or duet at the demand of the audience, is today almost nonexistent outside of Italy. Conductors like Arturo Toscanini and Vittorio Gui crusaded against the encore, only allowing it if there was no chance of the audience permitting the continuation of a performance otherwise, although Toscanini in one such circumstance actually just left the theater. Dramatically, the encore makes no sense. One doesn't repeat an aria or solo for any proper reason other than to show off one's singing or to play to an adoring public. One of the only instances in which singers managed to justify it dramatically was when Marcella Sembrich at the old Met, after singing the Letter Duet in *Figaro* with Emma Eames, would show the audience ink blots on the letter as the reason for repeating her "dictation." Still the encore lives and once in a while today it will surface in an unexpected place. Herbert von Karajan, a notedly authoritarian conductor, allowed an encore of the *Lucia* sextet in a famous Callas performance in the 1950s. Some composers, however, write an encore into the score, notably Sir Arthur Sullivan, who included them in *H.M.S. Pinafore, The Mikado* and others of the Savoy operas.

Similar to the encore is the nonsense that sometimes takes place in performances of *The Barber of Seville*. In the second act Rossini wrote a lovely "singing lesson" aria for Rosina, the soprano heroine. Almost from its premiere, however, singers have substituted whatever they've felt like singing. Ranging from "Home Sweet Home" or "Swanee" to the *Lucia* "Mad Scene," Handelian oratorio and the like, such interpolations are equally out of place, if by now traditional. In Johann Strauss's *Die Fledermaus* there is the famous party scene that has often tempted opera companies to produce sideshows; a recent transatlantic telecast of *Fledermaus* from Covent Garden featured a ballet divertissement and piano and violin virtuosi.

But sometimes audiences won't accept anything less. They've paid their money for entertainment, and some oddities have become obligatory to ensure such entertainment. There was a time when Adelina Patti, the Queen of Song for most of the last half of the nineteenth century, insisted that no matter what opera was performed, it be followed with a piano wheeled out onto the stage so that she could sing the inevitable "Home Sweet Home."

CHAPTER NINE

Opera myths and misconceptions

Throughout its long and glittering history, opera has been the public victim of countless myths and misconceptions. Although many prime donne have been among the most beautiful and glamorous women of their eras, and more recently even successful movie stars, some people avoid opera for fear of being devoured by a huge lady carrying a spear and sporting breastplates. To them, opera means violence, gore and bore. They have no desire to come any closer to opera than perhaps the old Marx Brothers movie *A Night at the Opera*, whose wild scenes will only confirm their worst fears about the art. Others see opera as remote and inaccessible, attended by a frigid, elite crowd in black tails, jewels and costly gowns.

These myths are often as colorful as opera's real history. It simply amounts to "bad press," but it can obscure the real facts about opera. It should be useful to examine some of these myths here, including the most amusing ones.

This writer has often been asked, "Do operas ever end happily? Is anyone alive at the final curtain?" Perhaps the ques-

tioners have only heard about operas like *Il Trovatore* by
Verdi, a very bloody piece which opens with a tale about a
baby thrown into a fire and ends with fratricide. It's these sensational operas that have always gotten the most publicity. But
there are just as many, if not more, charming operas with
happy endings; and they are not only the comic operas, but
some dramatic ones as well. In the stirring masterpiece *Fidelio*,
Beethoven's only opera, the heroine Leonore rescues her husband from a long imprisonment and impending death. It ends
in a paean of joy, reminiscent of the great composer's Ninth
Symphony. And of course comic operas rarely contain any violence. *Le Nozze di Figaro* by Mozart, *The Barber of Seville* by
Rossini, *Falstaff* by Verdi and *Don Pasquale* by Donizetti are
among the most popular operas ever written and they all end
happily, with the boy getting the girl and everyone surviving at
the conclusion.

The image of the fat prima donna in breastplates is one
which follows all opera singers. They appear on television talk
shows and, if they're slim, are inevitably asked, "Aren't opera
singers thinner and more attractive today?" The singers usually
respond with pride that, yes, singers are thinner today than the
legendary fatsos of the past and are much better actors, too. As
far as one can determine, these same statements were made as
early as within the first fifty years of the invention of opera and
have been made during every generation of the last two hundred years.

A story often told to support and foster this belief is the true
one of the world premiere of Verdi's *La Traviata* in 1853. The
heroine who sang the role of the delicate Violetta, a slim and
enchanting courtesan, was a huge prima donna and the audience was convulsed at the spectacle of this healthy, well-fed soprano dying of consumption. What is not so widely reported
is that the opera was shortly thereafter made popular by a
beautiful, slim and fascinating singer named Marietta Piccolomini, whose charm and not her voice won the day.

The fact is, there have always been singers who could sing
and not act, and singers who could act and not sing. Once in a
very great while there are singers who can both act and sing.

PLATES 30 AND 31. *Hermann Jadlowker, outstanding tenor of the early years of this century, and Adelina Patti, most famous of prime donne, belie the myth of the "fat singer."* (Author's collection)

But there have always been beautiful prime donne and handsome male singers as well as the unattractive ones, whose singing had to be great enough to compensate for their often preposterous appearance.

Marietta Alboni, for example, the great contralto of the early nineteenth century, was called by Rossini "the elephant who swallowed a nightingale," but her contemporaries Mario and Giulia Grisi were the preeminent tenor and soprano, as well as the handsomest stage couple, of the Romantic era. Henriette Sontag, a favorite of Beethoven and Weber, was so beautiful that duels were fought over her. On the other hand, the most popular tenor of today and the star of many of the Metropolitan's televised performances is much heavier than the legendary Enrico Caruso, the leading tenor at the Met from 1904 to 1921, or his predecessor Jean de Reszke, who was celebrated for his handsome stage appearance during his heyday in the 1880s and 1890s.

Many singers have been actors of such ability that they have been compared to the great actors of their day. Giuditta Pasta, the celebrated soprano for whom Bellini wrote his masterpiece, *Norma,* was called "the singing Siddons," a reference to Sarah Siddons, considered the greatest actress in the history of the English theater. At the end of the nineteenth century Emma Calvé, the fabled French soprano, still remembered as the definitive Carmen, was compared to the great Duse and not found to be her inferior.

More recently the ravishing American soprano Geraldine Farrar was Cecil B. De Mille's first star in a series of popular silent movies. Feodor Chaliapin, the famous Russian basso of the turn of the century, made an extraordinary film of *Don Quixote.* And of course glamorous Grace Moore and the magnetic Ezio Pinza were as famous on Broadway as at the Metropolitan.

Today there are more distinguished opera stars who are just as at home in movies, television, or on Broadway, and they will still probably claim to be the first slender singers who can act.

One very amusing myth is that the baritone never gets the girl. Most likely this story was originated by tenors and bassi.

Actually there are plenty of operas where the baritone is successful in love. The most famous is *Le Nozze di Figaro*, in which Figaro, traditionally played by a baritone, triumphantly overcomes all obstacles and wins his girl. In Puccini's *La Bohème*, it's the tenor who loses his love, Mimì, while the baritone ends up with the charming Musetta.

Among these widespread misconceptions, there are some which are native to America. Despite early and significant successes in the arts, America has always felt culturally inferior to the older European nations. Thus there have always been, almost from the time of the first American opera singers in the early 1800s, many fallacies about our own singers.

It is still widely believed that an American singer can't "make it" without studying and triumphing in Europe first. That this has never been true is demonstrated by the career of America's first true opera star, Clara Louise Kellogg. Born in South Carolina in 1842, this soprano made her debut in New York in 1861 and quickly became a national favorite. She numbered among her admirers such notables as Abraham Lincoln and General Sherman. She was an established star by the time she went to London, and successfully rivaled the beloved Adelina Patti. Later Kellogg sang in Russia with the most famous singers of the day, also to widespread acclaim.

Another singer who became world-famous before ever leaving America was the great Rosa Ponselle, acknowledged the leading soprano of the 1920s and 1930s. She made her debut opposite Caruso and reigned supreme on the Met's stage before she ever sang abroad. Born in St. Louis, Helen Traubel was very proud that she never sang in Europe, and she was the leading dramatic soprano of the 1940s.

Even more ludicrous is the claim that the American singers have been inferior or that they have only lately joined the ranks of the superstars. One would think that the careers of such singers as Ponselle, Kellogg and Traubel would be sufficient proof to the contrary. But despite these indisputable facts, every generation brings one or two singers who are then called the first American this-or-that, finally an American star the equal of the great European stars. In the 1900s it was

PLATE 32. *An American, Rosa Ponselle became a queen of prime donne without benefit of European training. (Author's collection)*

Geraldine Farrar, in the 1930s Lawrence Tibbett, and more recently Leontyne Price and Beverly Sills. So even though the American singer has been holding his or her own for 150 years, it will probably not be long before another singer is brought forward as the first great American opera singer with a world-wide reputation.

In a curious twist, America's attitude toward its most famous opera house is quite different from its attitude toward its singers. Americans firmly believe that the Metropolitan Opera is the greatest in the world and that it has always been so. There is a prevailing belief that the history of opera before the Met was less glorious and that the Met is the center of the opera universe.

It was the Met's great glory period of the first part of the century, which featured the great conductor Arturo Toscanini and the immortal Enrico Caruso, that gave the Met the prestige it still enjoys today. But despite the superlative performances which took place at the Metropolitan, it was still in some ways not the most important opera house in the world. In quality of performance it was exceptional, but not much more than other opera houses. A very important criterion for the stature of a house is the number of its world premieres. The most important premieres the Met has presented were *The Girl of the Golden West* by Giacomo Puccini and *Königskinder* by Engelbert Humperdinck during the season of 1910, perhaps the high-water mark in the history of the house. But consider that at about the same time operas like *Der Rosenkavalier, Elektra,* and *Ariadne auf Naxos* by Richard Strauss and *Le Coq d'Or* by Rimsky-Korsakov, were produced in other opera houses for the first time. These are far more important operas than those the Met premiered, and were produced with singers hardly less fabled than the great Met ensembles. Perhaps it was this reason which caused Toscanini to leave the Metropolitan in disgust in 1915. Toscanini knew that premiering works made an institution creative; away from the Met he conducted the first performances of *La Bohème, Pagliacci, Turandot* and *Nerone.* Certainly with Toscanini's departure the Met's musical superiority suffered a great blow,

PLATE 33. *The most important American opera house in the nineteenth century was not the Metropolitan Opera but the French Opera House in New Orleans, pictured above.* (Author's collection)

and when Toscanini later rejoined La Scala, that institution became superior to the Met in every way except for a few superstar singers still distinguishing the Metropolitan. During World War II the Met benefited from many celebrated conductors fleeing Hitler, but their overall influence on the artistic course of the house was minimal. Perhaps the old cliché about too many chefs was true, as the management had to divide the performance spoils among such truly fine conductors as Bruno Walter, Georg Szell, Fritz Busch and Fritz Reiner. Sir Thomas Beecham was on the roster as well, but after the war, these conductors all but disappeared from the Metropolitan and relative mediocrities took their places on a day-in and day-out basis, with star conductors present only as "guests." The critics have been complaining about the inferior conducting standards ever since.

Nothing is more illustrative of the Met's artistic decline since the days of Toscanini than the following tale of two tours. In 1910, Toscanini proudly brought his company to Paris, featuring such singers as Caruso, Hermann Jadlowker, Olive Fremstad, Frances Alda, Antonio Scotti and many other now legendary singers. Not surprisingly, the performances were an enormous success and left an impression which remained when the Met returned to Paris in 1966. This tour resulted in perhaps the most humiliating experience of the Met's history, especially on the opening night, which was marked by boos and calls for Maria Callas, who happened to be in the audience. Among all sorts of excuses made, some said that the company should have taken different productions and singers abroad. Others felt it was attributable to the anti-American feeling in France, which was admittedly very strong during that period of American involvement in the Vietnam War. The French critics declared that Paris had waited over fifty years for the Met to return, and they concluded that it had not been worth the wait.

Today, however, despite the unfortunate Paris fiasco, the Met is probably better than the Paris Opéra and equal to all of the other international giants. But it cannot claim any superiority over them, as the Metropolitan's productions and singers are the same one sees all over the world.

CHAPTER TEN

Three misunderstood terms and phrases

The Golden Age of Opera

When most people discuss a "golden age of opera," they are usually alluding to the period of Caruso's fame along with the great careers of Geraldine Farrar, Nellie Melba, Emmy Destinn, Antonio Scotti, Marcel Journet and others, roughly spanning the years of 1901–20. But there are three other periods which can justifiably be called golden and which are often misleadingly termed the "golden age of opera."

The two decades predating Caruso's reign at the Met were known as "the age of Jean de Reszke." This was the period of 1880–1901, which featured the legendary singers Adelina Patti, Marcella Sembrich, Francesco Tamagno, Victor Maurel, Mattia Battistini, Lilli Lehmann, Pol Plançon, Lillian Nordica and Édouard de Reszke, brother of the monarch of this period, the tenor Jean de Reszke. Critics were calling this the "golden age of opera" even while Caruso was singing. In the opinion of most critics who covered both periods, this earlier golden age was immeasurably superior to that of Caruso, as indeed the Polish tenor de Reszke was considered far superior to the Italian. At the Met and in London, "the nights of seven stars" were featured during the age of Jean de Reszke when stellar casts would be assembled for an opera such as *Les Huguenots*. The Met cast of January 8, 1896, included Nellie Melba, Lillian Nordica, Pol Plançon, Jean de Reszke, Jean Lassalle, Sofia Scalchi and Édouard de Reszke. Although if given the chance to pick a time to see opera many might choose the "de Reszke age," an even more remarkable generation preceded it.

The names of the great tenors who reigned during the heyday of romantic opera are often given to this age: Rubini and Mario. This is the period when the operas of Rossini, Bellini and Donizetti were created and performed by such singers as Giuditta Pasta, Maria Malibran, Giulia Grisi, Marietta Alboni, Henriette Sontag, Fanny Persiani, Gilbert Duprez, Adolphe Nourrit, Antonio Tamburini, Luigi Lablache and Jenny Lind, who came in at the end. Among the many highlights of this truly golden age was the world premiere of Bellini's *Norma* at La Scala in Milan on December 26, 1831, with Giuditta Pasta, Giulia Grisi and Domenico Donzelli in the cast. *Lucia di Lammermoor* by Donizetti was given for the first time in Naples in 1835 with the virtuosa Fanny Persiani, and Gilbert Duprez, the first tenor to sing a high C from the chest.

Another name given to this period is the "age of bel canto." This was the time of romantic opera and the groups of singers who dominated the age of bel canto were the quartets of the operas *Don Pasquale* by Donizetti and *I Puritani* by Bellini.

The legendary foursome that gave the first performance of *I Puritani* in Paris in 1835 was led by Giovanni Battista Rubini, the fabled virtuoso tenor; Giulia Grisi, the leading soprano of the age; Antonio Tamburini, who was said to have a fabulous technique; and Luigi Lablache, the great basso considered by some critics as the supreme singer of the period. This group became known as the "*Puritani* Quartet."

The *Don Pasquale* quartet included Grisi, Tamburini, Lablache and Mario, the handsome tenor husband of Giulia Grisi at the premiere at La Scala in 1843. Mario was considered a worthy successor to Rubini in this famous "*Pasquale* Quartet."

As great as the age of bel canto certainly was, there is one previous age which seems to have been, vocally at least, the most spectacular of all. During the "age of the castrati," scores with incredibly difficult vocal music were written by Handel, Gluck, Vivaldi, Telemann, Mozart, Piccinni and others. Sometimes referred to as *musici*, the castrati had techniques which, based on contemporary criticism and the evidence of the scores, appear to far outdistance those of any singers who followed them. These singers included the fabulous Farinelli, Caffarelli, Senesino and Carestini. The famous prime donne of the period were Faustina Bordoni and Francesca Cuzzoni.

Naturally distance makes everything seem more golden. For all of the confusing terminology of "golden age," it would appear that any group of singers which inspired and created great operas can be called golden. No doubt we will look back on singers like Len Cariou and Angela Lansbury, creators of *Sweeney Todd*; Julie Andrews and Rex Harrison, creators of *My Fair Lady*; Mary Martin and Ezio Pinza, creators of *South Pacific*; and others as members of a "golden age."

The discriminating opera buff will make certain of which golden age is referred to; don't hesitate to amaze your listeners by mentioning the "*Puritani* Quartet" or the "golden age of the castrati."

Bel Canto

Bel canto is a greatly abused and misunderstood term. Literally it means "beautiful song," but the term refers to much more than that. It originated with the high art of the castrati, although it's not even certain it was used then. Really only by the end of the nineteenth century were critics describing the art of Adelina Patti and others as examples of the "lost art of bel canto," thus bringing the term into fashion.

If we are not sure of when the term was first used, we do know what it refers to. It stands for the classical Italian

method of singing, especially as established by the great singing teacher Nicola Porpora, whose pupils Farinelli and
Caffarelli dominated the eighteenth century, and his followers,
Manuel Garcia, father and son, and Francesco Lamperti and
his son Giovanni. This art of bel canto flourished with the
refined singing demanded by the music of the period and
meant a combination of beautiful tone, phrasing, a perfect
trill, the artistic use of gradations of volume and coloration, and
especially the art of ornamenting or decorating the vocal line
with the above techniques. With some peaks and low points
through the years, the art of bel canto has been in a slow but
steady decline ever since the end of the castrati, the last of
whom sang as late as the early twentieth century.

One clear peak was the singing of the Romantic age which is
now more identified with the term bel canto than is the age of
castrati. The so-called age of bel canto is exemplified by the operas of Rossini, Bellini, Donizetti and the early works of
Meyerbeer. The singers of this tradition included Rubini and
Tamburini, for whom Bellini wrote such difficult roles, calling
all of the bel canto techniques of shading and ornamentation
into play, and which are now all but beyond the skills of any
living singer, male or female. Bel canto's final end came at the
end of the nineteenth century with the advent of the school of
opera known as verismo, and its vocal emphasis on volume
over finesse. Of late, there has been a well-publicized "bel
canto revival" through the efforts of Maria Callas and Joan
Sutherland. But modern male singers have proved woefully inadequate in bel canto style and technique. Actually the legendary Spanish contralto Conchita Supervia and the French soprano Lily Pons both revived bel canto operas in the 1930s
with conspicuous success twenty years before the activity of
Sutherland and Callas. While modern sopranos continue to
preserve a semblance of bel canto in theory and practice, the
males continue to ignore the trend, making a ludicrous imbal-
ance in the performances of the bel canto works. Even the
wholesale cutting of male roles, deplorable in itself, leaves
music far beyond the vocal abilities of most of the men. Fortunately, a new generation, including Kurt Moll, Renato Bruson,

Peter Schreier and others, has begun to show signs of developing skills in singing which may soon be comparable to their soprano contemporaries, leading to hopes for a true bel canto revival in the near future.

Coloratura

In many ways related to bel canto, coloratura too is a very misunderstood term. While it is correct to describe a soprano who can sing florid or bel canto roles as a coloratura soprano, most people wrongly believe that this is the only way in which the term "coloratura" can be applied.

Actually the word "coloratura" can properly precede tenor, basso, or baritone. There once were many notable coloratura tenors; Rubini was the most famous of them, but some more recent examples include Caruso's contemporaries John McCormack and Hermann Jadlowker, Strauss's favorite tenor, who possessed an extraordinary technique.

Unfortunately, singers and singing teachers alike appear to be ignorant of this fact and have subsequently influenced opera history. The term "coloratura" simply means an ability to sing florid music and can be applied to any voice category; but ask someone to name a coloratura and chances are it will be Lily Pons or Joan Sutherland. While these famous soprani are emulated by aspiring students, no one seems to be interested in emulating Tito Schipa or Cesare Valletti, tenors of the recent past with fair coloratura ability. Almost without exception, tenors want to imitate Mario Del Monaco or Franco Corelli and shout themselves hoarse. The tenors who do sing bel canto operas are trained to do so in a highly simplified manner, robbing the music of its sparkle and vivacity. As mentioned above, there has been some sign of a turnaround. One day, perhaps, Dick Cavett or Johnny Carson will introduce Mr. X, the sensational coloratura tenor, baritone or basso, or we will find him in a performance of *Lucia di Lammermoor* singing the coloratura of Edgardo, or as a bel canto Méphistophélès in *Faust*.

Reading about opera

It's a natural inclination for the operagoer to be curious about what others think of the quality of the performance and the opera he or she has seen or may be about to see. There is a lot of material available to satisfy one's curiosity on the subject. Beyond the immediacy of a newspaper or magazine review, there are a number of excellent reference books written about opera history and the works of specific composers. These include the excellent *The World of Opera* by Wallace Brockway and Herbert Weinstock, a fine general survey which is critical enough to be interesting, and the classic work of *Mozart's Operas* by Edward J. Dent. Similar books are available on Puccini, Verdi, Donizetti, Wagner and other composers and their works. References can be found that approach the subject from several different angles: performance history, history of singers and singing, musicology, stories of operas and history of opera houses, to name a few. Such books are often the best and most informed guides or histories of opera and a list of the most useful will be found at the conclusion of this section.

Publications

To some extent the history of an opera that interests you at
the moment will be covered in the review you consult concerning the quality of the performance you plan to or have already
attended. Many people wait until the first performance of an
opera and make their decision whether or not to attend after
reading the reviews. Reviews are found in the daily newspapers
as well as weekly magazines. They are found in monthly periodicals also, specifically those devoted exclusively to opera,
Opera News and *Opera*, of international circulation. The scope
of reviews will vary greatly, since in the daily papers critics are
usually meeting a deadline and will have to hurry the writing
of them. They write advance material, such as background and
history, before the performance and fill in the rest later. In
their haste they may sometimes not even catch the last act, a
source of irritation to opera management. Aware of this problem, the New York *Times*'s editorial policy is for the critic to
write the review for inclusion in the edition of the second day
after the performance. This gives completeness and objectivity
to the review, but also makes the news a little old.

Criticism is a very subjective thing. Ideally, a critic should be
familiar with the subject and have a background of attending
many operas and a fair knowledge of performance history and
the history of singing. Yet as basic as these requirements would
seem to be, it is sadly true that few critics even on the major
journals possess these credentials. And given any two critics
with excellent knowledge, ability and experience, the review
each may write of the same performance is often quite
different from the other. The decision is ultimately made by
the reader; it is imperative to remember that the critic is only a
guide and a reference.

In some cases, of course, criticism can be downright absurd,
as in the case of the critic who reviews a performance by
Nicolai Gedda in these terms: "The serenade was stylishly delivered, but his habit of turning every little phrase into an exer-
cise in good diction and beautiful singing is getting a bit tire-
some." This bit of sophistry appeared in a major daily and

proves that you must be careful to take all criticism with a grain of salt. Every critic has some ax or another to grind; unfortunately, they wield a great deal of power in doing so. To get the most out of them, you should read the reviews to compare them with your own reactions and impressions. If a critic seems to have made good sense to you and has agreed in past writings with the record of your own experiences, then you have found, for yourself, a reliable critic. Sometimes a particular journal will have a definite overall editorial inclination which, when recognized, can be a useful yardstick as well.

The main function of the reviewer of a performance is to comment on the quality of the production and the individual participants. A brief word of background can be welcome, but some critics get so carried away with musicological zeal that they bury the review in a mountain of obscure opera history. Certain critics even boast of the many different performances of an opera they have seen over the years and review them almost as thoroughly as the performance in question. While some of that can be extremely interesting, it is best saved for autobiographies or performance histories. Journalism should be concise; it should deliver only that information the reader wants and needs to know.

Aside from the daily newspapers in your town, the best way to follow the happenings of opera is through the special magazines devoted to the subject. The two major English publications are *Opera News* and *Opera*.

The older and better of the magazines is *Opera News*, published by the Metropolitan Opera Guild. This magazine is weekly during the broadcast season and monthly in the off-season. It is tailored for the Met's Saturday matinee broadcasts and serves its subscribers as a sort of "program of the air." At one time this was the chief function of *Opera News*, but the magazine has become considerably more than that. Today *Opera News* covers the national and international opera scene through reviews, gossip and critiques of books and recordings. Generously illustrated, it also features in-depth articles, some centering on the weekly Met broadcast and others on opera history in general. Issues of special interest include the United

States Opera Survey and Summer Festival issues. While one might question the validity of the reviews considering the magazine's ties to the Metropolitan Opera, the surprising fact is that the magazine is as independent as possible under the circumstances. Recently it has printed some shockingly negative reviews of certain Met activities, an encouraging trend. This must be credited to a courageous editorial staff, although certain individual reviewers are not as knowledgeable as the reader has the right to expect. While there is room for improvement among these and some of the specialized critics, the magazine is definitely getting better and better.

Opera is published in England by Harold Rosenthal, the editor, and is a magazine with many virtues. It is well laid out and its coverage of European events is far more extensive than that of *Opera News*. On the other hand, in covering activity in the United States, *Opera* is usually so far behind in time that its reviews are old news. It too has a good gossip section and reviews books and records. Each autumn an extensive Festival Issue is published by *Opera*. The emphasis of course is on performances in England; but *Opera* is perhaps most unreliable when discussing those same performances, as all too often some of their critics seem to be more interested in defending performances than in reviewing them. Why this posture exists is rather inexplicable, since performances in England are on such a high level. Too, *Opera* has been accused by more than one expert of a chauvinistic attitude toward native singers. This has resulted in the inflated reputations of several poor singers. All of these factors should then be borne in mind when reading this otherwise excellent publication; patriotism does seem to be a definite editorial policy.

For subscriptions and information write to:

Opera News	Opera
Metropolitan Opera Guild	D.S.B.,
1865 Broadway	18a The Broadway
New York, NY 10023	Wickford
	Essex SS11 7AA
	England

A Basic
Reference Library

In addition to newspapers and periodicals, an interesting way to learn about opera is to read some of the large quantity of books written about it. Along with the numerous books about composers and critical analyses of their operas, there are the various surveys of opera history, histories of opera houses and biographies and autobiographies of opera singers. While some of the singers' autobiographies are admittedly fanciful, they are almost invariably colorful, with unique insights into the world of opera and opera singing.

The following is a very select bibliography of the best of the books available, books that are necessary in making up a truly representative reference library. This bibliography is equally an essential reading list.

General Reference

The World of Opera, The Story of Its Development and the Lore of Its Performance, by Wallace Brockway and Herbert Weinstock, published by Modern Library, New York, 1941, 1962, 1966, is a marvelous critical history of opera. The performance annals are invaluable for research.

A Concise History of Opera, by Leslie Orrey, Scribner, New York, 1972, is a nice small history of opera with excellent illustrations. There is less criticism in this book, making it somewhat less interesting reading than the Brockway/Weinstock survey. The basic information is here nonetheless.

The Victor Book of the Opera, Simon & Schuster, New York, 13th edition, 1968. The Victor Books have since 1912 been the classics for opera stories and photographs of performers and productions. The stories of all the standard repertory operas are generally well synopsized; this thirteenth edition upholds the long tradition.

Composers' Biographies and Analyses of Their Operas

Vincenzo Bellini, by Herbert Weinstock, Alfred A. Knopf, New York, 1971, is the standard work on a composer Weinstock particularly admired.

Donizetti and the World of Opera in Italy, Paris and Vienna in the First Half of the Nineteenth Century, by Herbert Weinstock, Pantheon, New York, 1963, is a fascinating book with a great deal of opera history, as well as the best biography in print of the unfortunate composer.

Mozart's Operas, a Critical Study. . . , by Edward J. Dent, Oxford, London, 1913, is the classic analysis of the composer's operas, with an excellent, concise biography as well.

Famous Puccini Operas, by Spike Hughes, Dover, New York, 1972, a revised republication of the London, 1959 edition, is a very good survey of the works of the popular verismo master.

Rossini, a Biography, by Herbert Weinstock, Alfred A. Knopf, New York, 1968, completes Weinstock's trilogy of biographies of the bel canto composers, a task Weinstock was ideally suited for.

Verdi, His Music, Life and Times, by George Martin, London, 1965, is a good biography that provides useful information on Verdi's operas.

The Life of Richard Wagner, by Ernest Newman, London, 1947, is still the best work on the composer, although four volumes may prove tedious reading.

Critical Histories

Thirty Years Musical Recollections, by Henry Chorley, London, 1862, is a fascinating guide to the performances and singers of the first half of the nineteenth century by a crotchety but expert critic.

Vienna's Golden Years of Music, by Eduard Hanslick (edited by Henry Pleasants), Simon & Schuster, New York, 1950, will prove a revelation to many who know of this great nineteenth-century critic only through his bitterly satirical portrait by

Richard Wagner as Beckmesser in *Die Meistersinger von Nürnberg*. Hanslick was considered the foremost music critic of the century, respected by Brahms, Verdi and others. His criticisms make for interesting reading.

The Metropolitan Opera, 1883–1966, by Irving Kolodin, Alfred A. Knopf, New York, 1966, is an entertaining history of the Met, a definitive survey of its importance and tradition. The combination of history and critical analysis is penetrating and informative as written by the distinguished critic of the *Saturday Review*.

Celebration, The Metropolitan Opera, by Francis Robinson, Doubleday & Company, Inc., Garden City, N.Y., 1979, is a lavish photo book of the new Met, with interesting insights and amusing backstage stories. Some photos and history of the old house are featured as well. Magnificent photographs destine this book to be a collector's item, if it ever goes out of print.

Biographies and Autobiographies of Singers and Conductors

Alda, Frances. *Men, Women and Tenors*. Houghton Mifflin, Boston, 1937. A very amusing and interesting memoir by a soprano who often sang with Caruso.

Caruso, Dorothy. *Enrico Caruso, His Life and Death*. Simon & Schuster, New York, 1946. A warm and loving memoir of the legendary tenor by his wife.

Damrosch, Walter. *My Musical Life*. Scribner, New York, 1923. A pioneer musician in the United States, Damrosch gave very early performances of opera in this country. This autobiography is full of choice anecdotes of the great singers of his time.

Farrar, Geraldine. *Such Sweet Compulsion*. The Greystone Press, New York, 1938. This is a very popular book; despite its strange, "Ouija board" style, it is a colorful and informative view of that most glamorous of prime donne.

Flagstad, Kirsten. *The Flagstad Manuscript*. (Transcribed by Louis Biancolli) G. Putnam's Sons, New York, 1952. The frank autobiography of the most celebrated Wagnerian diva of this century.

Glackens, Ira. *Yankee Diva, Lillian Nordica and the Golden Age of Opera*. Coleridge Press, New York, 1963. The finest biography written of the greatest singer America ever produced.

Kellogg, Clara Louise. *Memoirs of an American Prima Donna*. G. Putnam's Sons, New York, 1913. Trenchant and observant autobiography of America's first celebrated singer.

Lauw, Louisa. *Fourteen Years with Adelina Patti*. La Scala Autographs, Plainsboro, N.J., 1977 reprint of the 1884 edition. A fascinating social history of the early years of the legendary Queen of Song.

Lehmann, Lilli. *My Path Through Life*. New York, 1914. A stupendous autobiography by the autocratic diva who helped Richard Wagner rehearse the first performances of the *Ring* cycle.

Merrill, Robert, with Sanford Dody. *Once More from the Beginning*. Macmillan, New York, 1965. Good autobiography by the popular American baritone with excellent insights into his work with Toscanini.

Pinza, Ezio, with Robert Magidoff. *An Autobiography*. Rinehart & Co., New York, 1958. Fine if slightly fanciful and highly expurgated story of the life of the great opera basso and Broadway star.

Ponselle, Rosa, and James A. Drake. *The Autobiography of Rosa Ponselle*, Doubleday & Company, Inc., Garden City, N.Y., 1981. At last, the long-hoped-for memoirs of the great diva have been published and have proved well worth the wait. Full of insight and anecdotes along with an excellent discography by William Park, this book is a "must" on any opera lover's reading list.

Sachs, Harvey. *Toscanini*. Lippincott, New York, 1978. At last, after all of the inaccurate, inadequate and inane books about this great conductor, here is a first-rate biography which puts the career of the most influential conductor in history into perspective.

Traubel, Helen. *St. Louis Woman*. New York, 1959. Candid

autobiography of the outstanding Wagnerian soprano of the 1940s.

Walter, Bruno. *Theme and Variations*. New York, 1946. A warm and informative life of the great conductor, with revealing facts about Gustav Mahler and his approach to opera, the Salzburg Festival, as well as Walter's own approach to Mozart, Verdi and opera in general.

Collected Biographies

The Great Opera Stars in Historic Photographs, by James Camner, Dover, New York, 1978, has 343 photos with brief biographies, from Tamburini and Jenny Lind to Tito Gobbi and Licia Albanese.

The Castrati in Opera, by Angus Heriot, London, 1956, is a fascinating book about the surgical wonders of the opera world.

The Great Singers, by Henry Pleasants, Simon & Schuster, New York, 1966, is an entertaining, light survey of the history of opera singing and singers.

The reader is advised to avoid *The Record of Singing*, published in three volumes by Duckworth in England. This could and should have been a useful book, but is unfortunately written from a very hostile point of view and concerns itself with ignorant criticism of singers.

Opera Libretti

Libretti of almost all the operas in the repertory are available from many different sources, but a notable series was published by Dover which includes a translation, a biography of the composer, musical notes and illustrations. They include *Carmen* by Bizet, *La Bohème* by Puccini, *Lucia di Lammermoor* by Donizetti, *Don Giovanni* by Mozart and *Aida* by Verdi.

Many of the books listed in this small bibliography are out

of print. They can often be found in local out-of-print book-shops or from mail-order firms. Information can be obtained by writing:

La Scala Autographs
P.O. Box 268
Plainsboro, NJ 08536

The Ballet Shop
1887 Broadway
New York, NY 10023

May and May
5 Hotham Road
London, S.W.15 1QN
England

APPENDIX II

Opera on record

Once the opera enthusiast has sampled live operas in the theater he may want to consider buying some recordings for enjoyment at home. Opera on records is never a substitute for live opera, but it is possible with a comparatively small outlay to have the complete standard repertory, including many works which otherwise can only be seen through many years of attending performances in houses all over the world. One can even buy recordings of works which may never be done on a modern stage, though they are masterpieces. Given the number of recordings available, it can be hard to choose correctly in building a nice library, without ending up with a "clinker" or an unwanted recording. The following will help you to invest wisely and avoid the "duds."

A basic opera record library should contain most of the standard repertory pieces as well as ones which ought to be in the repertory but aren't for reasons known only to impresarios. It is also possible to document the history of singing and performance practice through records, and the second part of this discography will list an essential historical record library.

Recordings on these lists are chosen using the following criteria: the work should be a "must" without which any library would be incomplete, the performance should be as distinguished as possible and, lastly, the sound should be adequate enough not to detract from the performance. Sound quality is of least importance, in our judgment, because what good is better fidelity in a poor performance, if all it does is let you hear bad singing or conducting more clearly? Thus, there are several pre-stereo recordings included for their overwhelming superiority as a musical experience. Another potential problem with many recent opera recordings, despite superior sound, is a lifeless result from antiseptic studio conditions and the inordinate amount of splicing, or patching together of different takes. Maria Callas was very sensitive to this and rarely allowed splicing in her recorded performances. It's very important to acquire recordings which can be replayed with lasting enjoyment countless times, and the handsome but lifeless "all-star" recordings which are flooding the market today may quickly lose their charm while, for instance, the incandescent Toscanini performances taken from live broadcasts remain ever fresh.

A Basic Opera Library on Record

BEETHOVEN, Ludwig van, *Fidelio*. The clear choice is the fine recording conducted by Otto Klemperer with Jon Vickers and Christa Ludwig on Angel S-3625. Also worthy of consideration is the performance by Toscanini on RCA LM-6025, which, despite an overmatched Rose Bampton as Leonore and inferior sound, allows Toscanini's classic interpretation to come through.

BELLINI, Vincenzo, *Norma*. In her first commercial *Norma* recording, Callas was a little closely miked, but her great performance is equaled by that of Ebe Stignani and the veteran conductor Tullio Serafin, on Seraphim 6037.

BELLINI, Vincenzo, *I Puritani.* The performance of Callas and Giuseppe Di Stefano remains the best, on Angel 3502.

BERLIOZ, Hector, *Les Troyens.* It was the conductor Colin Davis who was instrumental in restoring this great work to the standard repertory, and he has recorded the opera with Jon Vickers on Philips 6709002.

BIZET, Georges, *Carmen.* "Callas is Carmen" proclaimed the ads when this recording was released in the 1960s, and even though she never sang the role on stage, there was little disagreement. There is a good supporting cast headed by Nicolai Gedda and superior packaging for this recording on Angel S-3650.

DONIZETTI, Gaetano, *Don Pasquale.* The recording on Seraphim 6084 is more than fifty years old and the sound, subsequently, is antique, but the performance is a treasure. Tito Schipa gives a lesson in lyric tenor style and the rest of the cast has the true Italian buffa manner.

DONIZETTI, Gaetano, *Lucia di Lammermoor.* Seraphim 6032 has three aces with Callas, Di Stefano and Tito Gobbi in this justly famous recording. The newer recording with Joan Sutherland and Luciano Pavarotti on London 13103 is more complete, but lifeless in comparison.

GIORDANO, Umberto, *Andrea Chénier.* Seraphim 6019 has a great "all-star" performance with the most celebrated tenor after Caruso, Beniamino Gigli. Gino Bechi and Maria Caniglia are stalwart in support. The sound is antique, but no other performance approaches this one for the rare combination of excitement and smoothness.

GLUCK, Christoph Willibald, *Orfeo ed Euridice.* London 1285 has a spectacular Orfeo in Marilyn Horne, in the version originally written for a castrato, or male soprano, and arranged in the nineteenth century for Pauline Viardot by Berlioz. Gluck himself adapted the opera for its French premiere, because of the French aversion for castrati, and reset the role for a tenor. A fine recording of this slightly different opera, *Orphée,* is on Philips PHC 2-014 with a very distinguished performance by Léopold Simoneau and wonderful conducting by Hans Rosbaud.

GOUNOD, Charles, *Faust*. This is a choice between a classic performance in poor sound and a terrible performance in great sound. Actually, the classic performance, on Club 99 OP1000, has decent enough sound, considering the year it was made—1931. It features a Méphistophélès, Marcel Journet, who sang the role opposite Caruso in legendary days. He gives a sensational performance, combining Gallic charm and Mephistophelean menace along with an excellent trill in the serenade. The stereo versions offer casts that, for the most part, couldn't care less about what language they are singing, especially the Slavic bassos Boris Christoff and Nicolai Ghiavrov, whose lack of elegance would have made Gounod shudder.

LEONCAVALLO, Ruggiero, *Pagliacci*. The tenor is everything in this opera, and Seraphim SER 6009 has a vintage performance by Beniamino Gigli.

MASCAGNI, Pietro, *Cavalleria Rusticana*. London 12101 has Jussi Bjoerling, Ettore Bastianini and Renata Tebaldi in an unusually fine stereo recording, capturing a real "in house" atmosphere.

MASSENET, Jules, *Manon*. Seraphim 6057 has a reasonably Gallic performance, conducted by Pierre Monteux with Victoria de los Angeles as the coquette.

MEYERBEER, Giacomo, *Les Huguenots*. "All-star" performances of this opera were once a feature of the Golden Age of opera eighty years ago. Probably the closest performances to those nineteenth-century "nights of seven stars" were during the legendary La Scala revival in 1962, which featured Joan Sutherland, Giulietta Simionato, Fiorenza Cossotto, Franco Corelli, Vladimir Ganzarolli, Nicolai Ghiaurov and Giorgio Tozzi in the Italian version *Gli Ugonotti*. One of the live performances of that revival is preserved on MRF-18. Sutherland later participated in a complete recording in French on London 1437, but with a vastly inferior supporting cast and conductor.

MOZART, Wolfgang Amadeus, *The Abduction from the Seraglio (Die Entführung aus dem Serail)*. The superb recording conducted by Karl Bohm on DGG 270951, with its beautifully integrated cast, is especially distinguished by the great basso Kurt Moll, who actually trills in his arias. These discs prove that fine new stereo recordings are possible and one hopes for more of the same.

MOZART, Wolfgang Amadeus, *Così Fan Tutte.* Turnabout THS-6512 6/8, made in 1935, is the first recording of this opera and features the still unsurpassed, landmark Glyndebourne Festival performance. This is one of the most influential recordings ever made, as it helped initiate a Mozart revival all over the world, and the reasons for it are quite audible. RCA FRL 3 3639 has a great Fiordiligi in Kiri Te Kanawa paired with the fine Dorabella of Frederica Von Stade, but the men are barely adequate, making this recording only a good stereo runner-up.

MOZART, Wolfgang Amadeus, *Don Giovanni.* Philips PHI-670722 is the best of the crop with the great conductor Colin Davis, and a great singer in Kiri Te Kanawa as Donna Elvira. But the Don, Ingvar Wixell, though a fine singer, is undistinguished. London 1434 has the only distinguished Don since WW II in Cesare Siepi, and a few other good singers as well, but the conductor Josef Krips is indifferent.

MOZART, Wolfgang Amadeus, *Idomeneo.* This opera, composed by the twenty-five-year-old Mozart, is lesser-known than some of his others, but it is the greatest opera seria ever written and contains some of his finest music. Seraphim S-6070, an early stereo recording, has the pioneer Glyndebourne performance with two excellent singers in Léopold Simoneau and Sena Jurinac and a fine conductor in John Pritchard. A later recording on Philips 839758/60 is one of the poorest in the Colin Davis-Mozart opera series. The great conductor is not in top form and is burdened with a poor cast, especially in George Shirley, who is totally out of his depth in the title role.

MOZART, Wolfgang Amadeus, *The Magic Flute (Die Zauberflöte).* Deutsche Grammophon 2709017 is the choice with a good performance led by Karl Bohm, featuring the great tenor Fritz Wunderlich as Tamino.

MOZART, Wolfgang Amadeus, *The Marriage of Figaro* (*Le Nozze di Figaro*). Unfortunately, there is no recording of perhaps Mozart's greatest opera which can be recommended. The best of the lot, Philips 6707014, at least has as conductor Colin Davis.

MUSSORGSKY, Modest, *Boris Godunov*. This is the Russian opera to have in your library and Seraphim 6101 with Boris Christoff finds the Bulgarian basso in exemplary form for a role very well suited to his talents. Do not confuse it with the later recording of a similar cast in better sound but poorer form, Angel S3633.

PUCCINI, Giacomo, *La Bohème*. RCA VICS 6019-E has the definitive performance of the live broadcast by Toscanini (who conducted the world premiere in 1896), with Jan Peerce and Licia Albanese. Francesco Valentino, Anne McKnight and Salvatore Baccaloni complete the splendid cast.

PUCCINI, Giacomo, *Madama Butterfly*. Angel S-3702 is as good a performance as any, but all are very fine.

PUCCINI, Giacomo, *Tosca*. Angel 3508 is the Callas recording with Di Stefano, Gobbi and the conducting of Victor de Sabata, one of the most famous opera recordings in history.

ROSSINI, Gioacchino, *The Barber of Seville* (*Il Barbiere di Siviglia*). RCA LSC 6143 is a faithful re-creation of the fine Met performances of the 1950s and benefits from Cesare Valletti's elegant artistry and the solid contributions of Robert Merrill and Roberta Peters.

ROSSINI, Gioacchino, *William Tell*. The complete performance on Angel 3793 is one of the most notable commercial opera recordings of recent times. This immensely important work was the first "grand" opera and influenced the course of opera history. Nicolai Gedda turns in an admirable performance and Montserrat Caballé is in especially fine voice.

STRAUSS, Richard, *Der Rosenkavalier*. The performance on COL D4M 30652 with Christa Ludwig, Lucia Popp and Walter Berry, conducted by Leonard Bernstein, is the

choice of the complete recordings, but it lacks the magic
of the old abridged recording, featuring definitive performances by Lotte Lehmann, Elisabeth Schumann and Richard Mayr, great in the role of Baron Ochs, available on
Seraphim 6041.

STRAUSS, Richard, *Salome*. Strauss's erotic masterpiece is
given a vivid performance on Angel SBLX-3848 with the
excellent singer Hildegard Behrens in the title role. For an
even more exciting *Salome* experience most will be
satisfied with the music of the final scene (the best music
in the opera), which is fabulously performed by Ljuba
Welitsch on HMV-HLM 7006.

VERDI, Giuseppe, *Aida*. It is ironic that there are no satisfactory recordings of this very popular opera. The best is
the Toscanini-conducted performance on RCA VIC 6119,
which, in addition to the Maestro's incomparable conducting, has a good performance from Richard Tucker. The
performances of the Robert Shaw Chorale and the NBC
Symphony add much to the recording, but all of the other
principals are very poor. Some other recordings have better
all-round casts, but they are marred by inferior conducting.

VERDI, Giuseppe, *Falstaff*. The Toscanini recording on RCA
LM 6111 is one of the treasures of recorded opera. No
other performance comes within miles of this tribute by
Toscanini to his friend and idol, Verdi.

VERDI, Giuseppe, *La Forza Del Destino*. This is a blood and
thunder opera whose spirit is best served, despite some
cuts, by the raw power and vitality of the old Cetra
LP5-3236 recording with the brilliant-voiced Galliano Ma-
sini, Carlo Tagliabue (in his best recording), Tancredi
Pasero (best Italian basso after Pinza) and the wonderful
Ebe Stignani. A good stereo version, but without the fire
of the above, is RCA LSC 6413, which features the youthful soaring Leonora of Leontyne Price, Richard Tucker
and Robert Merrill.

VERDI, Giuseppe, *Otello*. At the world premiere of *Otello*,
an already famous conductor volunteered to play cello in

order to participate and learn at the feet of the master, Verdi. This was Arturo Toscanini, who years later brought his authority and genius to the broadcast of *Otello* recorded on RCA LM 6107, which combines the superb Otello of Ramon Vinay, the fabulous NBC Symphony Orchestra and the Robert Shaw Chorale. This peerless performance is a landmark in recorded opera.

VERDI, Giuseppe, *Rigoletto.* The famous Rigoletto of Leonard Warren is on RCA AVM 2-0698. Erna Berger and Jan Peerce round out the fine cast.

VERDI, Giuseppe, *La Traviata.* The finest recorded performance of this opera is the Toscanini-led recording on RCA LM 6003. He had the benefit of the Met's most famous Violetta of the time, Licia Albanese, and the fine youthful voices of Jan Peerce and Robert Merrill. Toscanini's conducting revitalizes this old chestnut, which all too often can drag under a poor conductor.

VERDI, Giuseppe, *Il Trovatore.* Despite a mediocre conductor, RCA AVM2-0699 is the compelling choice with Jussi Björling, Leonard Warren and Zinka Milanov in fine form.

WAGNER, Richard, *Der Fliegende Holländer.* The profound performance led by Otto Klemperer on Angel SCL 370 featuring the noble Dutchman of Theo Adam is the clear choice in a mediocre field.

WAGNER, Richard, *Lohengrin.* There are, unfortunately, no recordings which can be recommended. Any choice from the few in the catalogue will do as well as another until a decent recording appears.

WAGNER, Richard, *Die Meistersinger.* The recording by Herbert von Karajan on Angel SO3776 is a good one. This is Wagner's most "human" opera and will often please those who do not like his other works.

WAGNER, Richard, *Der Ring des Nibelungen.* The complete *Ring* conducted by the legendary German conductor Wilhelm Furtwängler is available on Seraphim 6100 on nineteen records, made from a live performance. This is a considerable investment and you may wish first to sample

Furtwängler's better-sounding studio recording of *Die Walküre* (the second opera in the *Ring* series) on Seraphim 6012.

WAGNER, Richard, *Tannhäuser*. The legendary Bayreuth Festival performance with the great Maria Müller and the extraordinary, superior Bayreuth Orchestra of prewar days is preserved on the recording made in 1930 in the Festival house itself. The extraordinary acoustics of the auditorium gave it a sound far advanced of the day and the recording is still quite serviceable. It is on EMI-IC-137-03130/32M.

WAGNER, Richard, *Tristan und Isolde*. The famous live recording from the 1966 Bayreuth Festival is on DG 2713001. This is a thrilling performance with an inspired Karl Böhm conducting and Birgit Nilsson at her very best. The only flaw is the pathetic Tristan by the "voiceless wonder," Wolfgang Windgassen. To get an idea of what Tristan should sound like, there is the special recording of the 1941 Met broadcast of *Tristan und Isolde* with Lauritz Melchior and Kirsten Flagstad. (The Metropolitan Opera Guild offers this and other legendary broadcasts for $125 each.)

WEBER, Carl Maria von, *Der Freischütz*. It's odd that this wonderful opera is almost never performed outside of Germany, although it introduced the age of Romanticism and changed opera history. It can be enjoyed on Ser-6010, a good performance.

WOLF-FERRARI, Ermanno, *Il Segreto di Susanna*. This enchanting comic opera by the last master of that genre is given a good recording on London 1169.

Related Works

The proper basic opera library should also have a small representation of operetta and musicals, which, while not grand opera, are nonetheless lyric theater. The following would constitute the minimum necessary to complete your opera record library.

GERSHWIN, George. *Porgy and Bess.* The Houston Grand Opera production which made opera history is documented on RCA ARL 3-2109.

GILBERT, William S., and SULLIVAN, Sir Arthur. *The Gondoliers.* London 12110 has the fine D'Oyly Carte performance of perhaps Sullivan's finest score. A joy.

GILBERT, William S., and SULLIVAN, Sir Arthur. *The Mikado.* London 1201 is the best stereo performance of their masterpiece, one of the greatest works of its kind in Western art. Avoid the inferior performance on London 12103.

GILBERT, William S., and SULLIVAN, Sir Arthur. *The Pirates of Penzance.* This popular favorite is the "American" G&S opera, as it received its world premiere here. The performance on London 1277 is the one to have, featuring a fine D'Oyly Carte cast.

GILBERT, William S., and SULLIVAN, Sir Arthur. *Yeomen of the Guard.* This is the closest G&S came to grand opera and a beautiful work it is. London 1258 has a good D'Oyly Carte performance.

OFFENBACH, Jacques. *La Grande-Duchesse de Gérolstein.* This sparkling operetta is given a fine performance on Columbia M2-34576 marred only by the tired singing of Régine Crespin.

OFFENBACH, Jacques. *Orphée aux Enfers.* A spectacular performance of this work on Angel SZX-3886 is one of the finest French performances of any opera to be put on record since WW II.

SONDHEIM, Stephen. *Sweeney Todd.* The most important musical of the 1970s, an unmistakably operatic work, is available in an outstanding original cast recording on RCA CBL2-3379.

STRAUSS, Johann. *Die Fledermaus.* Odyssey Y2-32666 preserves the historic English-language performance given at the Met in the 1950s featuring a scintillating performance by Ljuba Welitsch, Richard Tucker and Lily Pons.

After you've acquired the recordings in this basic list, you will have a foundation on which you can add many other

worthy recordings. In addition to other operas by the above
composers, you may wish to consider those by Daniel-François
Auber, Adrien Boieldieu, Luigi Cherubini, Domenico Cimarosa, George Frideric Handel, Saverio Mercadante, Giovanni Paisiello, Jean-Philippe Rameau and Gasparo Spontini.

A Library of Historic Performances

There are very few lovers of classical music who do not
dream about what it would be like to hear Beethoven play his
own concertos, or hear a legendary castrato sing Handel. Unfortunately, short of the invention of a time machine, this
won't happen, but one can hear on records the performances
of many participants in world premieres of legendary operas. It
is possible to hear the original singers for whom Verdi wrote
Otello and *Falstaff*. Almost all of the singers who created Puccini's operas left recordings, as well as some of the singers who
participated in Wagner premieres.

There is another great value in these old historic recordings;
they preserve not only a great singer's art, but a vanished style
as well. They give us a glimpse into a time when many male
singers had techniques more advanced than, say, Joan Sutherland's. The once great French school of singing has completely
disappeared from the stage, but the finest exponent of that
school, Pol Plançon, made fine recordings of his art. It can be a
revelation to hear these recordings. Music which can sound
dull and routine takes on new life with the imaginative singing
of these artists of the past.

Not long ago, this list would have represented a majority of
the recordings available, but now it is only a fraction of the
many historic issues, as many fine, small record companies,
mushrooming almost overnight, have inundated the market
with them. It is not our purpose to list all of the excellent and
worthy historical reissues, but to compile a representative
sampling of the art and style of the greatest of the historic
singers on record. Often these recordings were made under
primitive conditions, and if you cannot accept some scratches

and surface noise or anything less than high fidelity, then it might be best not to acquire them. But it is worth "listening through" the noise, for the rewards are great. It is only through these records that a proper idea can be formed of great singing. Those who have heard the fine tenor Luciano Pavarotti, called "better than Caruso" by some, will listen to Caruso himself and form their own conclusions. They will encounter the art of a basso who will dazzle them with a coloratura capability unheard today. And they will hear a singer of whom Verdi, when asked who were his three favorite sopranos, responded, "Adelina, Adelina and Adelina." This was Adelina Patti, whose Gilda in *Rigoletto* caused the composer to weep with joy.

BATTISTINI, Mattia. Battistini is unquestionably the greatest baritone on records. The recital of eighteenth- and nineteenth-century arias on "Mattia Battistini, Vol. 1," Perennial 3001, gives an ample demonstration of his art and is especially valuable for its lesson in bel canto singing. His handling of the recitative in "Là ci darem la mano" is a revelation.

CARUSO, Enrico. "Immortal Performances 1904–1906," Victrola VIC 1430, is perhaps the best single LP of Caruso to date. Here is the young Caruso at the top of his career, but also at his lyric best. Avoid the so-called improved, computer-processed recordings on RCA.

CHALIAPIN, Feodor. Seraphim 60218 and Seraphim 60211 show the unique genius of this most famous of Russian singers. He was not a bel canto stylist, but his individualistic and dramatic singing triumphs. He will always be considered the definitive Boris Godunov.

DELLER, Alfred. The recital on L'Oiseau-Lyre 01S 109 is not an old record; in fact, it is a fine stereo recording. But it is historic as a document of the art of the man who brought the countertenor back to popularity after three hundred years.

DE LUCIA, Fernando. The recording of excerpts from *Il Barbiere di Siviglia* on Rubini SJG-121 is one of the most valuable historic reissues, for the bel canto demonstration De

Lucia gives in style and the use of ornamentation to underline the comedy is eye-opening. As the role was originally created by a legendary, virtuoso tenor, Manuel Garcia, it is especially valuable to have a coloratura treatment of this music for the first time on LP.

DEVRIÈS, David. Club 99 39, "David Devriès," has amazing singing, especially in the aria from *La Dame Blanche* where the tenor consecutively trills higher and higher into a superb head voice. His French diction and style are a balm to all lovers of French opera.

GALLI-CURCI, Amelita. The recital on Victrola VIC 1518 is a wonderful demonstration of the warm and gentle art of this beloved soprano. Some of the recordings on this LP were called perfect by no less an authority than Geraldine Farrar, and we agree.

HESCH, Wilhelm. The recital on Court Opera 300 of the most outstanding German basso on records is spectacular. His deep voice begins to descend into rich low notes where other bassi leave off. That he can essay fluent runs and trills as well is final proof that coloratura is not a female exclusive. His recordings of the arias from *Entführung* are possibly the closest we will ever come to the art of the legendary Ludwig Fischer, for whom Mozart wrote the role.

JADLOWKER, Hermann. The Everest Scala SC 839 recital reveals an extraordinary tenor who could have given Caruso, or even Nellie Melba, lessons. Possessing the most perfect trill on records, Jadlowker dazzles with coloratura and also gives impressive performances of such heavy dramatic roles as Otello. The aria from *Idomeneo* is perhaps the most spectacular record ever made of a Mozart aria. On Rubini GV62, one is amazed to hear the aria from *Tannhäuser* sung with fluid runs as it was meant to be.

McCORMACK, John. The art of another superb tenor is revealed on Victrola VIC 1472, which has the definitive performance of "Il mio tesoro," one of the most famous vocal recordings in history; RCA VIC 1393 has the equally impressive "Oh sleep, why dost thou leave me?"

MELCHIOR, Lauritz. The art of this "Caruso of Wagnerian tenors" is well demonstrated on the impressive recording of *Die Walküre,* on Seraphim 60190, with Lotte Lehmann and conducted by Bruno Walter.

NORDICA, Lillian. The legendary accomplishments of America's greatest singer is documented on a recording available from the Nordica Homestead, Holly Road, Farmington, Maine 04938, for a $10 donation. This issue has all of the soprano's records, which are of variable quality, but good enough to show what a stupendous singer she was.

PATTI, Adelina. There is ample evidence to support the conclusion that Patti is the greatest soprano in operatic history, and her faded but still effective art is featured on the EMI set C147-01 500/01, which contains all of her known records. There is an indescribable charm in hearing a Stephen Foster song rendered by a soprano who was his contemporary. The *Sonnambula* recording is the next best thing to being in a time machine for the glimpse it gives us of the authentic Romantic style by this favorite of Rossini. Her poise and trill are perfect, and the strength and personality of the old lady will surprise those who expect to hear cold coloratura.

PINZA, Ezio. Pinza's recital on Victrola VIC 1418 preserves the most beautiful basso voice on records. Pinza's noble art featured superlative diction and fine acting, with a personality of unrivaled magnetism.

PLANÇON, Pol. Pol Plançon was considered by contemporary critics to be the flawless vocal artist of the Golden Age of opera during the 1880s and '90s, and records featured on Rubini GV 39 made at the end of his career give ample proof of this assertion. Such suave and elegant singing combined with a fabulous technique and deeply felt characterizations add up to some of the most treasured recordings ever made. Along with the recordings of David Devriès, they serve as examples of the lost French style.

PONSELLE, Rosa. The recital on Victrola VIC 1507 has several fine recordings by one of America's most legendary singers. She has been called the female Caruso, but was possibly even finer. Her perfect singing line and absolute poise made her an ideal Norma.

RETHBERG, Elisabeth. Toscanini called this contemporary of Rosa Ponselle's the perfect soprano, and, indeed, her voice is perhaps the most beautiful soprano on records. Her noble and intense style made her the Aida of her time and Victrola VIC 1683 has the complete Nile Scene from that opera, as well as arias which highlight her great artistry.

SCHUMANN-HEINK, Ernestine. One of the most beloved singers in history, as well as the greatest contralto on records, Schumann-Heink's art can be sampled on Victrola VIC 1409. The richness and depth of her voice will astound and amaze the listener; her virtuosity is unexcelled.

SUPERVIA, Conchita. The recital on Seraphim 60291 of the great Spanish mezzo-soprano reveals a singer of true genius. Gifted with a personality perhaps even more powerful than Chaliapin's and a stunning technique, her records blaze forth with tremendous impact, a revelation of the art of bel canto. Her recording of "Nacqui all'affanno" from *La Cenerentola* is probably the finest Rossini recording ever made.

TAMAGNO, Francesco. Though his recordings on EMI C065-00658 were made at the time this great tenor was dying, they are still stupendous. Verdi wrote *Otello* for him and there is little doubt that this is the most thrilling voice ever to sing the role. With the unique, clarion peal in his voice, he was a fine stylist as well, using ornamentation and grace notes to advantage. This voice, which purportedly rocked chandeliers in many opera houses, was considered one of the wonders of the world; there is plenty of evidence on this record to reveal that as an understatement.

While most of the complete operas listed earlier can easily be found in almost any good record store, many of the private labels like MRF and some of the historic records can be hard to find. However, the following people should be able to provide the harder-to-find recordings on this list:

MRF RECORDS, P.O. Box 26, Bogota, NJ 07603. Although this is a private label, their quality of production (they use the same record manufacturers as major labels) is superb. They provide scholarly librettos with each recording and have an unrivaled repertory of unusual and important operas. Their Cherubini series is especially recommended.

WILLIAM VIOLI, 1231 60th Street, Brooklyn, NY 11219. Mr. Violi puts out a list featuring historical reissues, private recordings of rare operas and out-of-print LP's and 78's. He can find almost any record for a customer.

Chronology of important events

Opera	World History
1594	
The first opera, *Dafne*, by Jacopo Peri, is performed.	Henri IV of France is crowned at Chartres; *Love's Labour's Lost* is written by William Shakespeare.
1607	
Orfeo by Claudio Monteverdi, the first operatic masterpiece, is performed.	Pocahontas saves Captain John Smith of the newly founded Jamestown colony in Virginia.
1642	
Monteverdi's *L'Incoronazione di Poppea* premieres in Venice.	Civil War begins in England; Rembrandt van Rijn paints *The Night Watch*.
1674	
Jean-Baptiste Lully's *Alceste* premieres in Paris.	The drama *Iphigénie* by Jean Racine is performed at Versailles.

1689

Dido and Aeneas, the great   William and Mary assume
English opera seria of Henry   the English monarchy.
Purcell, is performed.

1702

The first opera performed in   The last of the Stuart
America is presented in   monarchy, Queen Anne,
Charleston, South Carolina.   ascends the English throne.

1705

The greatest of the castrati   Isaac Newton is knighted by
and the most legendary   Queen Anne.
singer in history, Farinelli, is
born.

1724

Julius Caesar by George   Rémy Martin Cognac is
Frideric Handel is premiered   introduced in France.
in London with the great
castrato Senesino.

1728

The Beggar's Opera, a ballad   Danish explorer Vitus Bering
opera satire on Handelian   discovers the Bering Strait.
opera by John Gay and John
Pepusch, is performed.

1733

La Serva Padrona by   Savannah is founded by
Giovanni Pergolesi is   James E. Oglethorpe in
performed in Naples,   Georgia.
heralding the popularity of
opera buffa; *Hippolyte et
Aricie* by Jean-Philippe
Rameau is premiered in Paris.

1756

Wolfgang Amadeus Mozart is born in Salzburg.	The Seven Years' War begins in Europe, and the French and Indian War breaks out in the North American colonies.

1762

Gluck's great reform opera *Orfeo ed Euridice* premieres in Vienna.	Catherine the Great becomes Czarina of Russia at the age of thirty-three.

1769

Fifteen-year-old Mozart's opera *La Finta Semplice* is performed.	Thomas Jefferson builds Monticello.

1776

The Bolshoi Theater is built in Moscow.	The American Revolution begins officially with the drafting of the Declaration of Independence.

1778

The most famous opera house in the world, Milan's Teatro alla Scala, is built.	The French recognize American independence, signing an alliance with Benjamin Franklin; Captain Cook discovers the Sandwich Islands.

1781

Idomeneo, Mozart's great opera seria, is premiered in Munich.	General Cornwallis surrenders at Yorktown.

1782

Mozart's great German Singspiel, *Die Entführung aus dem Serail,* is performed in Vienna.

An important early novel, *Cecilia,* by Fanny Burney, is published.

1785

Le Nozze di Figaro by Mozart is premiered in Vienna.

The dollar is established as the official currency of the United States.

1787

Don Giovanni by Mozart is performed for the first time in Prague.

The Constitution of the United States is written in Philadelphia.

1789

George Washington attends an opera in New York at the John Street Theater.

The Bastille prison in Paris is stormed by French peasants; George Washington is inaugurated as the first American President.

1791

Mozart's *Die Zauberflöte* is performed at Vienna's Burgtheater with success, but Mozart dies shortly thereafter.

The Bill of Rights is passed into U.S. law.

1814

The third and most successful version of Beethoven's only opera, *Fidelio,* is premiered.

Napoleon abdicates, retiring to the island of Elba; the "Star-Spangled Banner" is published by Francis Scott Key in a Baltimore newspaper.

1816

Rossini's great masterpiece, *Il Barbiere di Siviglia*, is premiered in Rome.

James Monroe becomes the President of the United States; *Emma* by Jane Austen is published.

1821

Der Freischütz by Carl Maria von Weber premieres in Berlin, adventing the Romantic era.

Napoleon dies on St. Helena; the electric motor is invented by Michael Faraday.

1835

I Puritani receives a brilliant premiere, but its composer, Vincenzo Bellini, dies shortly thereafter.

P. T. Barnum goes into show business for the first time.

1842

Giuseppe Verdi has his first great success with *Nabucco*.

The Oregon Trail is opened.

1850

P. T. Barnum brings Jenny Lind, the Swedish Nightingale, to America for a lucrative tour.

The first national Women's Rights convention in America is held at Worcester, Massachusetts.

1859

Faust by Charles Gounod is premiered, making Gounod the most popular opera composer of his time; the French Opera House, the first great opera house in America, is built in New Orleans.

Construction of the Suez Canal begins; Charles Dickens' *A Tale of Two Cities* is published.

1861

Performances of Wagner's
Tannhäuser result in the
infamous Jockey Club riot.

Civil War begins in the
United States.

1864

The brilliant operetta *La
Belle Hélène* by Jacques
Offenbach is premiered.

Sherman leads his "March to
the Sea" through Georgia.

1865

Tristan und Isolde by Richard
Wagner is produced for the
first time in Munich.

The American Civil War
ends; President Abraham
Lincoln is assassinated in
Ford's Theater.

1871

Aida by Verdi receives its
world premiere in Cairo,
Egypt; the first collaboration
of Gilbert and Sullivan,
Thespis, is performed at
London's Gaiety Theatre.

The Chicago fire devastates
the city.

1875

Carmen by Georges Bizet is
premiered in Paris.

Alexander Graham Bell
invents the telephone.

1876

The first complete production
of Wagner's *Ring* cycle opens
the first Bayreuth Festival.

The U.S. 7th Cavalry, led by
General George Custer, is
massacred at the Battle of
Little Big Horn.

1877

Edison invents the
phonograph.

Tchaikovsky's ballet *Swan
Lake* is premiered in Moscow.

1879

The Pirates of Penzance has its world premiere in America, with Gilbert present and Sullivan conducting.

F. W. Woolworth opens his first discount counter.

1883

The Metropolitan Opera House in New York is built.

The Brooklyn Bridge opens.

1886

Toscanini conducts his first opera in Rio de Janeiro.

Geronimo is captured by the U. S. Army, ending the last major Indian war.

1887

Verdi's great dramatic masterpiece, *Otello*, is premiered at La Scala.

Pratt Institute, America's first art college, opens in Brooklyn.

1893

Verdi's last opera, the comic *Falstaff*, is premiered.

Lizzie Borden is acquitted of the ax murders of her parents in Fall River, Massachusetts.

1894

America's great soprano, Lillian Nordica, is chosen to create the role of Elsa at the Bayreuth premiere of *Lohengrin*.

Dreyfus is sent to Devil's Island.

1896

Puccini's *La Bohème* is premiered in Turin, Italy, conducted by Toscanini.

Olympic games are revived in Greece.

1902

Enrico Caruso makes his first phonograph records in a hotel room in Milan.

Arthur Conan Doyle revives his popular detective, Sherlock Holmes, in *The Hound of the Baskervilles.*

1903

Enrico Caruso makes his debut at the Metropolitan Opera in *Rigoletto.*

The Wright brothers make their first successful flight at Kitty Hawk.

1908

Arturo Toscanini conducts his first performance at the Metropolitan Opera.

The Model T Ford automobile is produced for the first time.

1909

Arnold Schoenberg composes the atonal *Erwartung,* dealing a death blow to classical music; *Prince Igor* is presented by the Ballet Russe company, starring Feodor Chaliapin and introducing Diaghilev productions to Paris.

Robert Edwin Peary is the first man to reach the North Pole; the first kibbutz is settled in Palestine.

1911

Richard Strauss's masterpiece, *Der Rosenkavalier,* is premiered in Dresden.

The Manchu Dynasty ends in China, and Sun Yat-sen returns.

1917

Sigmund Romberg's *Maytime,* starring Peggy Wood, opens on Broadway.

The Russian Revolution begins; the United States enters World War I.

1927

Jerome Kern's *Show Boat* is premiered.

The Jazz Singer is the first talking picture.

1935

Porgy and Bess by George Gershwin is premiered.

Persecution of Jews in Germany begins in earnest with the Nuremberg Laws.

1941

Lady in the Dark, starring Gertrude Lawrence, with lyrics by Ira Gershwin and music by Kurt Weill, premieres on Broadway.

The United States enters World War II.

1943

Oklahoma! by Richard Rodgers and Oscar Hammerstein II revolutionizes the American musical.

The United States Marines take Guadalcanal; Mussolini is toppled and Italy surrenders to the Allies.

1966

The old Metropolitan Opera House is abandoned as the company moves to Lincoln Center.

Worldwide protests begin against U.S. involvement in the Vietnam War.

1978

Sweeney Todd, lyrics and music by Stephen Sondheim, is premiered on Broadway.

Israel and Egypt sign a peace treaty.

The language of opera, a glossary

APPOGGIATURA: The adding of an extra note as preparation for or pause before the main note.

ARIA: A set number or song in an opera, usually self-contained with an identifiable beginning and end.

BARITONE: The middle range of the male voice with a compass between low G and G two octaves above.

BASSO (Italian, *basso*=low): The lowest range and category of the male voice, ideally ranging from low E to the F two octaves above.

BEL CANTO (Italian=beautiful song): A term for a florid, or-namented style of music and singing, combined with a perfect legato. See Chapter 10, "Three Misunderstood Terms and Phrases."

BRAVO (Italian=hurrah): Praise for a performance; bravo is used to applaud a male; brava, a female; and bravi, more than one performer.

BUFFO (Italian=comedian): A male comic opera specialist; a clown in the theater.

CABELETTA: The second and more spectacular part of an aria. Originally this was just the *da capo*, or "from the beginning," repeat of an aria decorated by the singer, but composers eventually began writing specifically more florid second parts or repeats.

CADENZA: A florid ornamental passage optionally inserted by a singer before the last cadence or end of an aria.

CANTILENA: An almost archaic term for the smooth and flowing part of an aria or song.

CASTRATO (Italian=castrated): A male soprano or contralto whose voice was prevented from breaking in puberty by means of castration. Also known as *musici*, the castrati developed into singers of legendary brilliance and had a unique, "sexless" tone only approximated by a countertenor. There exist recordings, made in 1902, of the last of the castrati, Alessandro Moreschi, a second-rate church musician of limited vocal quality.

CLAQUE: A hired group of applauders.

COLORATURA: Florid vocal music. See Chapter 10, "Three Misunderstood Terms and Phrases."

COMPRIMARIO: A specialist in small character roles.

CONTRALTO: The lowest of the three categories of female voices, from F to G below middle C, extending upward for two octaves. True contralto voices are very rare.

COUNTERTENOR: A high male voice, using much head tone similar to, but essentially different from, a falsetto. The countertenor may be an alto or soprano in range, but should have a definite "male" quality, rather like that of a choirboy.

DIVA (Italian=goddess): A term that is synonymous with prima donna; a female opera singer.

FALSETTO: An unfortunately misleading term used to describe the high pitch of the voice caused by using only part of the vocal cords. When poorly done, the male falsetto may sound effeminate, which accounts for its infrequent use today. It is, however, the proper way to sing high notes in the bel canto operas. It may be heard on recordings of Hermann Jadlowker and John McCormack; see Appendix II, "A Library of Historic Performances."

FIORITURA (Italian=flowering): The ornamental line of singing, either written or improvised. A feature of the bel canto operas.

HELDENTENOR: The term for a heroic German tenor, usually with a deep baritonal quality in his voice, especially suited to Wagner's operas. Lauritz Melchior was the definitive heldentenor of this century.

LEGATO: Steadiness of emission and an evenly connected tone production.

LIBRETTO: The text of an opera.

MAESTRO (Italian=master): An honorary title for a great musician, most often applied to a conductor. During Toscanini's lifetime the term was synonymous with his name.

MESSA DI VOCE (Italian=placing of the voice): The technique of swelling and diminishing the tone on one note.

MEZZA VOCE (Italian=half voice): Singing at half volume, with a veiled effect.

MEZZO-SOPRANO: The middle range of the female voice. Many mezzi-soprani are actually "short" soprani who can't sing the highest soprano notes of C and above.

PORTAMENTO (Italian=carrying): The smooth gliding from one note to another over several notes at once, without breaking off during the transition.

PRIMA DONNA (Italian=first, or leading, lady): The soprano lead; a colloquial meaning is a capricious and willful opera soprano.

SOPRANO: The highest range of the female (or castrato) voice. There are several subcategories; a dramatic soprano sings such heavy, dramatic roles as Isolde or Leonore/Fidelio. The spinto soprano sings middle dramatic roles such as Elsa or Aida. The lyric soprano sings the lighter roles, including Gilda, Elvira and Zerlina. Other categories include soubrette, the comic light soprano, and the coloratura soprano, meaning a soprano singer of florid music.

TENOR: The highest range of the natural male voice. As in the soprano range, there are several categories. The dramatic tenor sings heavy roles such as Manrico, Radames and Florestan (see also Heldentenor). The lyric tenor sings such lighter roles as Ernesto in *Don Pasquale*, the Count in *Il Barbiere di Siviglia* and the Duke in *Rigoletto*. The less-used term of *tenore di grazia* means much the same as lyric tenor.

TREMOLO: The wobble or exaggeratedly out-of-control vibrato of the voice.

TRILL: The rapid alternation of two adjacent notes. The only proper trill will sound both notes clearly. Some singers merely sing a rapid staccato, interrupting the flow of air through the larynx, a very quick "cough" that is actually a pseudo-trill.

VERISMO: The Italian term for naturalism; the movement popular at the turn of the century, as practiced by Puccini, Mascagni, Leoncavallo, Giordano etc. It also refers to the style of singing verismo operas.

VIBRATO: All voices have a natural vibrato, or vibration, as the air passes through the larynx. Vibrato was often purposely heightened by bel canto singers for ornamentation. When totally out of control or too broad it is a tremolo. Singers with a distinctive vibrato were the nineteenth-century tenors Mario and Rubini, and, on records, the mezzo-soprano Conchita Supervia.

INDEX

Academy of Music, 88
Adler, Kurt Herbert, 93
Adrian (Hollywood designer), 137
Adults
    first operas for, 13–16
AIDA (Verdi), 6, 14, 34–39, 55,
        58, 77, 79, 137
    ballet, 56, 79
    "Celeste Aida," 35, 38, 55, 57
    ensembles, 55–56
    "Fuggiam, fuggiam," 38
    history and story, 34–39
    "Io resto a te," 37
    love arias, 55
    love duet, 55
    Nile scene, 55
    "O patria mia," 37
    orchestra, 57
    "O terra addio," 38
    overture, 56
    "Pur ti riveggo, mia dolce Aida,"
        37
    "Ritorna vincitor," 36
    Triumphal Procession, 36, 38
    vocal techniques, 57
Aida (soprano role in Aida), 36,
        37, 38, 55
Alboni, Marietta, 146, 154
Alceste (Gluck), 58
Alceste (Lully), 78
Alda, Frances, 151
Amahl and the Night Visitors
        (Menotti), telecast, 132
American Ballet Theatre, 80, 82
American musicals, 98

American opera, 94
American opera festivals, 100–7
American Opera Society, 125
American School of Ballet, 82
American singers, 147–48
Amneris (mezzo-soprano role in
        Aida), 36, 37, 38, 55
Amonasro (role in Aida), 36–37
Amor (role in Orfeo ed Euridice),
        52
Andrea Chénier (Giordano), 8
Andrews, Julie, 155
Anna Bolena (Donizetti), 89, 98
Annie, 98
Anselmi, Giuseppe, 114
Antony and Cleopatra (Barber), 9
Applause, 85
Arabella (R. Strauss)
    Houston Grand Opera
        production, 124
Aria, 2, 6, 7, 136
Ariadne auf Naxos (R. Strauss),
        149
Aspen Festival, 104
Atlanta, Metropolitan Opera
        national tour, 88, 104
Atlántida (Falla), 114
Atonal music, 8–9
Auber, Daniel-François
    La Muette de Portici by, 79
    Manon Lescaut by, 128
    Opera recordings, 125
Audience, 82–85
Australia, opera in, 114

Babes in Arms, 98
Baccaloni, Salvatore, 71, 118
Balanchine, George, 81, 82
Balfe, Michael William
  The Bohemian Girl by, 101
Ballad of Baby Doe, The (Moore), 101
Ballad operas, 7
Ballet, 56, 78–82
  Baroque, 3
  on point technique, 81
Balthrop, Carmen, 95
Baltimore Civic Opera, 100
Barber, Samuel, 9
  Antony and Cleopatra, by, 9
Barber of Seville (Paisiello), 114, 128
Barber of Seville, The (Rossini), 19, 22, 71, 127, 128, 141, 144
Baritones, 71
Baroque opera, 3, 118, 120, 135–36
Baroque style, 5
Bartered Bride, The (opera/movie), 130
Bassi, 4, 51, 71
Basso buffo (comic bass), 44, 71
Battistini, Mattia, 137, 153
Bayreuth Festspielhaus, 28
Bayreuth Festival (Bayreuth, Germany), 66, 103, 115–16, 121
  Parsifal, 116
  Ring cycle, 116
Beecham, Thomas, 73, 150
Beethoven, Ludwig van, 30, 64, 146
  Fidelio by, 74, 127, 128, 144
Beggar's Opera, The (Gay), 7
Bel canto operas, 66, 126, 154–55, 155–57
Bellini, Vincenzo, 125, 126, 127, 156
  Norma by, 108, 146, 154
  I Puritani by, 66, 154, 155
Benois, Alexandre, 77
Benois, Nicola, 77, 97
Benvenuto Cellini (Berlioz), 98

Berg, Alban, 8, 19
  Lulu by, 8, 19, 100
  Wozzeck by, 8, 19
Bergman, Ingmar
  The Magic Flute (opera/movie), 68, 119–20, 131–32
Berio, Luciano, 100
Berlin opera, 113
Berlioz, Hector, 52, 66
  Benvenuto Cellini by, 98
  Les Troyens, 90, 98
Berman, Eugene, 50
Bernstein, Leonard, 74
Bibbiena family, 2
Bing, Rudolf, 83, 118
Bizet, Georges, 7, 15, 66, 127
  Carmen by, 7, 15, 94
Bloch, Ernest
  Macbeth by, 92
Bohème (Leoncavallo), 128
Bohemian Girl, The (Balfe), 101
Bohemian National Opera (Prague), 113
Böhm, Karl, 74
Boieldieu, Adrien
  La Dame Blanche by, 127
Boïto, Arrigo, 138
Bolshoi Opera (Moscow), 113–14
Bomarzo (Ginastera), 19
Booing, 84
Bordoni, Faustina, 155
Borodin, Alexander
  Prince Igor by, 79
Boston, Metropolitan Opera national tour, 104
Box office, 8
Britten, Benjamin
  Peter Grimes by, 8, 9, 19
Broadway musicals, 9, 94
Brünnhilde (soprano in *Ring* operas), 58
  "Ho jo to ho" battle cry, 66
Bruson, Renato, 156
Burles, Charles, 67
Burlesque, 7
Burney, Charles, 65
  General History of Music by, 63, 64
Busch, Fritz, 118, 150

Caballé, Montserrat, 68, 89, 125
Caccini, Giulio, 2
Caffarelli (castrato), 155, 156
Caldwell, Sarah, 97–98
Callas, Maria, 67, 89, 98, 127, 137,
    141, 151, 156, 172
Calvé, Emma, 146
Calzabigi, Ranieri, 5, 52, 55
Camden Festival, 126
Camille (Dumas fils), 14
Capobianco, Tito, 76, 96,
    103
Capriccio (R. Strauss), 92–93
Carestini (castrato), 155
Cariou, Len, 11, 155
Carmen (Bizet), 7, 15, 94
Carson, Johnny, 157
Carousel, 9
Caruso, Enrico, 66, 67, 73, 88,
    114, 130, 146, 147, 149, 151,
    153, 154
  My Cousin (opera/movie), 131
  as Radames in Aida, 35
Casanova, 44
Castrati, 4, 134–35, 155
Catalani, Alfredo, 8
Cavalleria Rusticana (Mascagni),
    8, 16
Cavalli, Pier Francesco
  L'Egisto by, 100
  opera recordings, 125
Cavett, Dick, 157
Central City Opera Festival, 101,
    107, 123, 138
Chagall, Marc, 110
Chaliapin, Feodor, 88, 114, 130,
    146
Cherubini, Luigi, 90, 110
  Les Deux Journées by, 127
  Medea by, 98, 127
  recordings, 125
Chicago Lyric Opera, 93–94, 106
Children
  first operas for, 16–18
Choreographers, 81
Christie, John, 117
Cimarosa, Domenico, 44
Cincinnati Opera, 98
Cincinnati Summer Opera Festival,
    104

City Center, 92
Claques, 84–85
Classical eighteenth-century opera
    seria, 73
Cleveland, Metropolitan Opera
    national tour, 88, 104
Cleveland Opera, 100
Colline (basso role in La
    Bohème), 24, 27
Coloratura, 66, 157
  rapid, 65
Columbia record company, 125
Comic bass (basso buffo), 44, 71
Comic operas, 4, 5, 6, 9
Comic operetta, 9
Commendatore (role in Don
    Giovanni), 44, 45, 49
Conductor, 72–75
Conrad, Richard, 66
Corelli, Franco, 137, 157
Corena, Fernando, 71
Corsaro, Frank, 76
Cosi Fan Tutte (Mozart), 58
Costumes, 2
  Baroque, 3
Countertenors, 66
Covent Garden (London), 107,
    111–13, 121, 129
  Die Fledermaus telecast, 141
Crispino e la Comare (Ricci
    brothers), 126
Cuzzoni, Francesca, 155

Dalayrac, Nicolas, 126
Dallas, Metropolitan Opera
    national tour, 88, 105
Dallas Civic Opera, 98
Dance/dancing, 2, 3, 7
Da Ponte, Lorenzo, 44, 138
Das Rheingold (Wagner), 18
Death scenes, 136
Debussy, Claude
  Pelléas et Mélisande by, 8, 19
Deller, Alfred, 66
Del Monaco, Mario, 137, 157
De Mille, Agnes, 79
De Mille, Cecil B., 70, 146, 149
Dent, Edward J.
  Opera by, 138
De Reszke, Édouard, 153

De Reszke, Jean, 28, 38, 88, 146,
    153, 154
Der Fliegende Holländer
    (Wagner), 76
Der Freischütz (Weber), 58
Der Rosenkavalier (R. Strauss),
    18, 134, 149
Designer, 76–78
Destinn, Emmy, 35, 88, 153
Detroit, Metropolitan Opera
    national tour, 88, 105
DGG record company, 125
Diaghilev, Sergei, 77
Dialogue, 7
Diamond Horseshoe, 139
Diction, 63, 67
Dido and Aeneas (Purcell), 81–82
Die Fledermaus (J. Strauss), 6, 7
    Covent Garden telecast, 141
Die Walküre (Wagner), 18
Die Zauberflöte. See The Magic
    Flute
Di Filippi, Arturo, 96
Dom Basilio (tenor role in Le
    Nozze di Figaro), 72
Domgraf-Fassbänder, Willi, 118
Domingo, Placido, 65
Don Giovanni (Mozart), 9–11, 18,
    44–51, 71, 113, 128
    "Ah! chi mi dice mai," 45
    ballet, 56
    "Batti, batti, o bel Masetto," 47
    "Catalogue Aria," 45
    "Champagne Aria," 47
    "Dalla sua pace," 47
    "Deh vieni alla finestra," 48
    ensembles, 55–56
    "Finch' han dal vino," 47
    "Ho capito, Signor, si!" 46
    "Il mio tesoro," 47, 49, 55, 57
    "Là ci darem la mano," 46, 55
    love arias, 55
    love duet, 55
    Metropolitan Opera production,
        50
    "Mi tradi," 49
    "Non mi dir," 50, 57
    "Notte e giorno," 44
    Opera buffa, 44, 51
    orchestra, 57

"Or sai chi l'onore," 47
    overture, 56
    patter song, 45–46, 49
    sets, 50
    story, 44–51
    tragedy/comedy arguments,
        43–44, 51
    "Vedrai, carino," 48–49
    vocal techniques, 57
Don Giovanni (bass or baritone
    role in Don Giovanni), 44–51
    passim, 56, 57
Donizetti, Gaetano, 125, 126, 156
    Anna Bolena by, 98
    Don Pasquale by, 5, 6, 71, 127,
        144, 154
    L'Elisir d'Amore by, 14, 16, 17,
        71
    Lucia di Lammermoor by, 6, 92,
        127, 136, 154, 157
    Torquato Tasso by, 126
Don Juan, 43, 46
Donna Anna (dramatic soprano
    role in Don Giovanni), 44–51
    passim, 55, 57
Donna Elvira (dramatic soprano
    role in Don Giovanni), 45–51
    passim, 55
Don Ottavio (tenor role in Don
    Giovanni), 46–51 passim, 55,
    57
Don Pasquale (Donizetti), 5, 6,
    71, 127, 144, 154
    quartet, 155
Don Quixote (opera/movie), 130,
    146
Donzelli, Domenico, 154
Drama, 2
Dramatic operas, 73
Dramma giocoso (humorous
    drama), 11, 43
Drottningholm Court Theater
    (Stockholm, Sweden), 3, 82
Drottningholm Festival
    (Drottningholm, Sweden),
    119–20, 122
Duets, 2, 6
Dumas, Alexandre, fils
    Camille by, 14

Dupre, Gilbert, 65, 154
Duse, Eleonora, 146

Eames, Emma, 28, 30
    Letter Duet with Marcella
        Sembrich, 141
Early classical opera, 118, 120
Early-nineteenth-century music, 65
Edinburgh Festival (Edinburgh,
    Scotland), 118, 121
Eisinger, Irene, 71
Elektra (R. Strauss), 149
Elisabeth (soprano role in
    Tannhäuser), 41, 42, 43
*Elixir of Love, The. See L'Elisir
    d'Amore*
Embellishment, 63, 65
EMI record company, 125
Encore, 140–41
England
    operetta, 6, 7
    comic opera, 9
English/foreign language attitude,
    137–38
English National Opera, 113, 138
Ensemble, 6, 55–56
Esclarmonde (Massenet), 90
European Opera festivals, 115–22
Everyman (Reinhardt/Salzburg
    Festival production), 117

Falla, Manuel de
    Atlántida by, 114
Falsetto, 65
Falstaff (Verdi), 35, 97, 137, 144
Farinelli (castrato), 134, 135, 155,
    156
Farrar, Geraldine, 69, 70, 73, 88,
    117, 130, 146, 149, 153
Farrell, Eileen, 127
Faust (Gounod), 8, 15, 28–34,
    110, 157
    "A toi l'enfer," 33
    "Avant de quitter," 30, 31
    ballet, 56
    ensembles, 55–56
    Flower Song, 31
    Garden Scene, 31, 55
    Garden Scene Quartet, 32
    history and story, 28–34

"Invocation," 32
Jewel Song, 32, 57
"Jugée," 34
"Le veau d'or," 31
love arias, 55
love duet, 55
Metropolitan Opera productions,
    28
orchestra, 57
overture, 56
"Salut, demeure, 31–32, 55, 57
Soldiers' Chorus, 33
vocal techniques, 57
"Vous qui faites l'endormie," 33
Walpurgis Night ballet, 33
Faust (tenor role in *Faust*), 30–34
    passim
Ferretti, Jacopo, 134
Festival Aix-en-Provence (Aix,
    France), 118–19, 121
Festival Ottawa, 104, 107
Fidelio (Beethoven), 74, 127, 128
First opera
    for adults, 13–16
    for children, 16–18
    to be avoided, 18–20
Florence. *See* Renaissance
    Florentines
Fracci, Carla, 101
Fremstad, Olive, 81, 151
French opera, 2–3, 8, 126, 127
    grand opera, 8, 22
    Music Academy, 67
    nineteenth century, 66–67
    operetta, 6
    seventeenth-century ballet, 78,
        79
French Opera House (New
    Orleans), 98, 150
Freni, Mirella, 68
Friends of French Opera, 126
Furtwängler, Wilhelm, 74

Galli-Curci, Amelita, 88
Garbo, Greta, 14
Garcia, Manuel (father and son),
    156
Garden, Mary, 130
Gay, John
    The Beggar's Opera by, 7

Gedda, Nicolai, 66, 125
General History of Music
   (Burney), 63–64
German opera, 127
   comic opera, 5
   dance in opera, 79
   grand opera, 3, 7
German romanticism, 39, 43, 58
Gershwin, George
   Porgy and Bess by, 9, 11, 94;
      telecast, 132
Giannini, Dusolina, 91
Gilbert, William S., 7
Gilbert and Sullivan, 7, 92
Ginastera, Alberto, 20
   Bomarzo by, 19
Giordano, Umberto, 7
   Andrea Chénier by, 8
Girl of the Golden West, The
   (Puccini), 19, 149
Gluck, Christoph Willibald, 5, 51,
   64, 80, 90, 125, 127, 136, 155
   Alceste by, 58
   Iphigénie en Aulide by, 58
   Orfeo ed Euridice by. *See Orfeo
      ed Euridice*
   overture, 56
Glyndebourne Festival
   (Glyndebourne, England), 71,
   117–18, 121
Gobbi, Tito, 72
Gockley, David, 94
Goethe, Johann Wolfgang von, 34
Golden age of opera, 153–55
Goldoni, Carlo, 128
Goldwyn, Samuel, 69
Goodspeed Opera House, 98, 99,
   106
Gounod, Charles, 8, 15, 16, 28,
   29, 30
   Faust by. *See Faust*
   overture, 56
   Roméo et Juliette by, 8, 16, 133
Grande Académie de Musique. *See
   Paris Opera*
Grand opera, 6, 7–9
   Belle Époque, 30
   French, 30
Grau, Maurice, 72

Greater Miami Opera Association,
   96–97, 106
Greek drama, 1
Greek mythology, 2
Grétry, André, 110
   opera recordings, 125
Grisi, Giulia, 146, 154
Grisi, Mario, 146, 154
Gui, Vittorio, 140

Halász, László, 91
Halévy, Ludovic, 6, 110
Hamlet (Shakespeare), 43
Hamlet (Thomas), 96
Hammerstein, Oscar, II, and
   Richard Rodgers, 9
Handel, George Frideric, 3, 4, 7,
   64, 136, 155
   Julius Caesar by, 3, 89, 91
   opera recordings, 125
   Rinaldo by, 124
Hänsel und Gretel
   (Humperdinck), 16, 133
   Metropolitan Opera production,
   17
Hans Heiling (Marschner), 127
Happy endings, 143–44
Harrison, Rex, 155
Hawaii, opera troupe, 100
Haydn, Joseph, 44, 127
   complete opera recordings, 125
Henderson, William J., 28
High notes, holding, 136–37
H.M.S. Pinafore, 141
Hoffmann, E.T.A., 43
"Home Sweet Home," 141
Homer, Louise, 53
Horne, Marilyn, 65, 124, 125
Houston Grand Opera, 94, 95,
   106, 123, 138
   Arabella, 124
   Porgy and Bess, 11
   Rinaldo, 124
Humorous drama (*dramma
   giocoso*), 11, 43
Humperdinck, Englebert, 7
   Hänsel und Gretel by, 16, 17,
   133
   Königskinder by, 149

Idomeneo (Mozart), 4, 56, 57, 58, 80, 91
Il Barbiere di Siviglia. See Barber of Seville, The
Il Campiello (Wolf-Ferrari), 5, 128
Il Crociato in Egitto (Meyerbeer), 126
I Lombardi (Verdi), 58, 103
Il Segreto di Susanna (Wolf-Ferrari), 6
Il Trovatore (Verdi), 14–15, 58, 103, 144
   Anvil Chorus, 15
   Intermezzi, 4
Iphigénie en Aulide (Gluck), 58
I Puritani (Bellini), 66, 154
   quartet, 154, 155
Ismail Pasha, 35
Italian grand opera, 7–8, 22, 127
   dance in, 79

Jadlowker, Hermann, 145, 151
Janáček, Leoš
   Jenůfa by, 20
Jenůfa (Janáček), 20
Joan of Arc (opera/film), 70
Jockey Club (France), 79
John F. Kennedy Center for the Performing Arts, 90, 100, 105
   Wolf Trap, 100
Jones, Robert Edmond, 78
Joplin, Scott
   Treemonisha by, 94, 95
Joseph (Méhul), 126–27, 128
Journet, Marcel, 153
Juilliard School, 92–93
Julius Caesar (Handel), 3, 77, 89, 91

Kanawa, Kiri Te, 68, 124, 139
Karloff, Boris, 38
Kellogg, Clara Louise, 147
Kelly, Lawrence, 98
Kennedy Center. *See* John F. Kennedy Center for the Performing Arts
Kenny, Yvonne, 126
Kern, Jerome
   Show Boat by, 9

Keyboard recitative, 5
King and I, The (Rodgers and Hammerstein), 9
Kolodin, Irving
   The Metropolitan Opera by, 74
Königskinder (Humperdinck), 149

La Belle Hélène (Offenbach), 7
Lablache, Luigi, 71, 154
La Bohème (Puccini), 8, 13, 14, 22–28, 58, 94, 128, 147
   "Addio senza rancor," 27, 55
   "Che gelida manina," 24, 25, 31–32, 55
   death scene, 136
   ensembles, 55
   history and story, 22–28
   love arias, 55
   Metropolitan Opera performances, 23, 26, 94
   "Mi chiamano Mimì," 24, 25
   Musetta's Waltz, 25, 26
   "O Mimì, tu più non torni," 27
   orchestra, 57
   "O soave fanciulla," 25, 55
   U.S. premiere, 26
   "Vecchia zimarra," 27
   vocal techniques, 56
La Clemenza di Tito (Mozart), 56
La Dame Blanche (Boieldieu), 127
La Fanciulla del West. See Girl of the Golden West
La Gioconda (Ponchielli)
   "Dance of the Hours," 79
Lake George Opera Festival, 104
La Loca (Menotti), 196
Lamperti, Francesco, 156
Lamperti, Giovanni, 156
La Muette de Portici (Auber), 79
Lansbury, Angela, 11, 155
La Scala, 9, 80, 84, 89, 100, 107, 150, 154
La Serva Padrona (Pergolesi), 5, 71
Lassalle, Jean, 28
La Traviata (Verdi), 14, 94, 113
   death scene, 136
La Vestale (Spontini), 127
Lawrence, Marjorie, 114

Le Bourgeois Gentilhomme
  (R. Strauss), 82
Le Coq d'Or (Rimsky-Korsakov),
  149
L'Egisto (Cavalli), 100
Lehár, Franz
  The Merry Widow by, 92
Lehmann, Lilli, 88, 153
  Salzburg Festival, 117
Lehmann, Lotte, 137
Leitmotiv (theme), 39
L'Elisir d'Amore (Donizetti), 14,
  16, 71
  Metropolitan Opera production,
  17
Le Nozze di Figaro (Mozart), 19,
  44, 50, 58, 72, 128, 131, 133,
  134, 144, 147
Leoncavallo, Ruggiero
  Bohème by, 128
  Pagliacci by, 8, 16, 28, 149
Leonora (Paër), 128
Leporello (basso buffo role in *Don
  Giovanni*), 44–51 *passim*, 56
Le Prophète (Meyerbeer), 6, 77
Les Deux Journées (Cherubini),
  127
Les Huguenots (Meyerbeer), 6, 89,
  90
Les Indes Galantes (Rameau), 78,
  82
Les Troyens (Berlioz), 90, 98
Le Temple de la Gloire (Rameau),
  78, 82
Libretto/libretti, 3, 5, 21–22,
  137–38
  translation, 137, 138–39
Light Opera of Manhattan, 92
Lincoln Center, 9, 88, 90–91, 92
  Mostly Mozart Festival, 104
Lind, Jenny, 154
"Live from Lincoln Center" PBS
  telecasts, 92
"Live from the Met" PBS
  television series, 71, 88
Lohengrin (Wagner), 6, 127
London record company, 125
Lone Ranger (radio and television
  series), 19
Lortzing, Albert, 128

Los Angeles, 23, 92
Louise (opera/movie), 130
Louis XIV, 3
Lucia di Lammermoor (Donizetti),
  6, 92, 127, 136, 154, 157
  sextet from, 6
Lucrezia Borgia, 89
Luisa Miller (Verdi), 90–91
Lully, Jean-Baptiste, 109, 110, 127
  Alceste by, 78
  opera recordings, 125
Lulu (Berg), 8, 19, 100

Macbeth (Bloch), 92
McCormack, John, 57, 66, 127,
  157
McCracken, James, 66
Madama Butterfly (Puccini), 8,
  14, 23, 58, 108
  "Un bel dì" ("One fine day"),
  14
Maeterlinck, Maurice, 138
Magic Flute, The (Mozart), 5,
  16–18, 19, 139, 140
  opera/movie, 68, 119–20,
  131–32
Mahagonny (Weill), 11
Mahler, Gustav, 73, 83–84, 88
Maievsky, André, 67
Malibran, Maria, 154
Man of La Mancha, 98
Manon Lescaut (Auber), 128
Manon Lescaut (Puccini), 58
Marcello (baritone role in *La
  Bohème*), 24–28 *passim*, 55
Margarethe, 34. See also *Faust*
Marguerite (soprano role in
  Faust), 30–34 *passim*, 57
Markova, Alicia, 81
Marriage of Figaro, The. See *Le
  Nozze di Figaro*
Marschner, Heinrich, 127
  Hans Heiling by, 127
Martha (role in *Faust*), 32
Martin, Mary, 155
Martin, Peter, 82
Martinelli, Giovanni, 35
Martin y Soler, Vincente, 50
  Una Casa Rara by, 128

Marx Brothers
  A Night at the Opera, 143
Mascagni, Pietro, 7
  Cavalleria Rusticana, by, 8, 16
Masetto (baritone role in *Don
  Giovanni*), 46–51 *passim*, 55
Massenet, Jules, 8, 125, 128
  Esclarmonde by, 90
Mathis, Johnny, 66
Maurel, Victor, 33, 153
Medea (Cherubini), 98, 127
Méhul, Étienne
  Joseph by, 126–27, 128
Meilhac, Henri, 6
Melba, Nellie, 88, 114, 153
  in *Faust*, 28
  as Mimì, 23
"Melba Night," 113
Melchior, Lauritz, 137
Melody, 9
Memphis, Metropolitan Opera
  national tour, 88, 105
Memphis, opera troupe, 100
Menotti, Gian Carlo
  Amahl and the Night Visitors
    (telecast), 132
  La Loca by, 96
  Spoleto festivals, 101, 120
Méphistophélès (basso role in
  Faust), 15, 30–34 *passim*, 57,
  157
Mercadante, Saverio, 126, 127
  recordings, 125
Merola, Gaetano, 93
Merrill, Nathaniel, 77, 90–91
Merry Widow, The (Lehar), 92
Metastasio, Pietro, 3, 138
Metropolitan Opera, The
  (Kolodin), 74
Metropolitan Opera House, 9, 11,
  18, 83–84, 88–91, 92, 94, 100,
  127, 138, 140, 146, 149–50
  Aida, 34
  and American Ballet Theatre, 82
  ballet, 81
  conductors, 72
  Der Fliegende Holländer, 76
  Der Rosenkavalier, 77
  Die Frau Ohne Schatten, 77, 78
  Don Giovanni production, 50

Faust, 28
"Faustspielhaus," 28
Hänsel und Gretel production,
  17
La Bohème, 23, 26, 94
L'Elisir d'Amore production, 17
Le Prophète, 77
"Live from the Met," 71
national tour, 88, 104–05
Orfeo ed Euridice production,
  53
Salome, 81
Tannhäuser production, 41, 116
telecasts, 129
Metropolitan Opera House (old),
  91, 139
Meyerbeer, Giacomo, 75, 77, 156
  Il Crociato in Egitto by, 126
  Le Prophète by, 6, 77, 80
  Les Huguenots by, 6, 89, 90
  opera recordings, 125
  Robert le Diablo by, 79
Mezzo-soprano voice, 133
Mikado, The, 141
Milnes, Sherrill, 96
Milwaukee Opera, 100
Mimì (soprano role in *La
  Bohème*), 23–28 *passim*, 55
Minneapolis, Metropolitan Opera
  national tour, 88, 105
Modern opera, 8, 19–20
Molière, 43
Moll, Kurt, 156
Monteverdi, Claudio, 4, 91
  opera recordings, 125
Moore, Douglas
  The Ballad of Baby Doe by, 101
Moore, Grace, 130, 137, 146
Mostly Mozart Festival, 104
Movies, opera in, 129–32
Mozart, Wolfgang Amadeus, 1, 30,
  64, 80, 90, 113, 155
  Cosi Fan Tutte by, 58
  Don Giovanni by. *See Don
    Giovanni*
  Glyndebourne Festival, 71,
    117–18, 121
  Idomeneo by, 4, 56, 57, 58, 80,
    91

Ingmar Bergman opera/movie, 68, 119–20, 131–32
  La Clemenza di Tito by, 56
  Le Nozze di Figaro by, 19, 44, 50, 58, 72, 128, 131, 133, 134, 144, 147
  The Magic Flute by, 5, 16–18, 19, 139, 140
  Mostly Mozart Festival, 104
  Salzburg Festival, 116–17, 121
Mozartean form, 44
Mozart of the Champs-Élysees, 6
MRF record company, 125, 127, 128
Mummy, The (movie), 38
Munich opera, 113
Murger, Henri
  Scènes de la Vie de Bohème by, 23, 28
Musetta (soprano role in *La Bohème*), 25, 26, 27, 55
Music, 2, 8
  atonal, 8–9
  orchestrated, 7
  tonal, 8
Music Academy (France), 67
Musicals, 9
Music drama, 7, 9, 39
Musici, 155
My Cousin (opera/movie), 131
My Fair Lady, 155

NBC Opera Theater, 132
Nerone (Boïto), 149
Newark, Opera troupe, 100
New Orleans Opera, 98
New York City Ballet, 80, 82, 92
New York City Opera, 11, 81–82, 91–93, 105, 138
  Julius Caesar unit set, 77–78
  New York State Theater, 92
  telecasts, 123
New York State Theater, 92
New York Sun, 28
Nicolai, Otto, 128
Night at the Opera, A (Marx Brothers movie), 143
Nilsson, Birgit, 118
Nordica, Lillian, 72, 88, 153
Norma (Bellini), 108, 146, 154

Nourrit, Adolphe, 154
Novotná, Jarmila, 130
Nureyev, Rudolf, 80, 82

Oberlin, Russell, 66
Offenbach, Jacques, 6, 67
  La Belle Hélène by, 7
O'Hearn, Robert, 77
Oklahoma! (Rodgers and Hammerstein), 9, 79
Olivero, Magda, 101
Opera (Dent), 138
Opera box, 139–40
Opera buffa, 5, 6, 22, 44, 51, 71, 73
Opéra-Comique, 126
Opera Orchestra, 125
Opera Rara, 125
Opera seria, 2, 3, 22, 44, 52
  Italian, 3
Opera Society of Boston, 97–98
Operetta, 6, 7
  comic, 9
Orchestra, 57, 58
  recitative, 5
Orfeo (castrato/contralto role in *Orfeo ed Euridice*), 52–53, 54, 136
Orfeo ed Euridice (Gluck), 5, 51–55, 80
  "All'amor voi ognor," 54
  "Amata mia sposa," 54
  ballet, 54
  "Che farò senza Euridice?" 54
  "Chi puro ciel," 54
  Dance of the Happy Shades, 54, 80
  "Deh placatevi con me," 52
  French version, 52
  "Gli sguardi trattieni," 52
  love arias, 55
  love duets, 55
  Metropolitan Opera production, 53, 81
  opera seria, 52
  orchestra, 58
  story, 52–55
  "Trionfi Amore," 54
  "Vien con me, o diletta," 55
  vocal techniques, 57

Orlando Furioso (Vivaldi), 98
Orphée et Eurydice, 52. *See also*
    Orfeo ed Euridice
Otello (Rossini), 128
Otello (Verdi), 6, 16, 35, 66, 108,
    128
Overture, 56

Pacific Northwest Wagner Festival,
    103, 107
    Wagner's *Ring* production, 102
Pacini, Giovanni, 127
    recordings, 125
Paër, Ferdinando
    Leonora by, 128
Pagliacci (Leoncavallo), 8, 16, 28,
    149
Painting, 2
Paisiello, Giovanni, 44
    Barber of Seville by, 114, 128
    opera recordings, 125
Pants roles, 133–34
Paradise Lost (Penderecki), 9, 94
Paris Opéra, 3, 79, 80, 89, 107,
    109–10, 151
    ballet, 110
Parsifal (Wagner), at Bayreuth,
    116
Pasta, Giuditta, 146, 154
Patter song, 45–46, 49
Patti, Adelina, 114, 126, 145, 147,
    153, 155
    as Aida, 137
    and Home Sweet Home, 141
Pavarotti, Luciano, 65, 68, 118
Pelléas et Mélisande (Debussy), 8,
    19
Penderecki, Krzysztof, 9
    Paradise Lost by, 9, 94
Pergolesi, Giovanni Battista
    La Serva Padrona, 5, 71
Peri, Jacopo, 2
Persiani, Fanny, 154
Personality, 72
Peter Grimes (Britten), 8, 9, 19
Philadelphia, Metropolitan Opera
    national tour, 88, 105
Philips record company, 125
Piccinni, Niccolò, 127, 155
    recordings, 125

Piccolomini, Marietta, 144
Pinza, Ezio, 51, 84, 140, 146, 155
Pittsburgh, opera troupe, 100
Plançon, Pol, 15, 28, 153
Ponchielli, Amilcare
    La Gioconda by, 79
Ponnelle Jean-Pierre, 131
Pons, Lily, 156, 157
Ponselle, Rosa, 38, 100, 127, 147
Porgy and Bess (Gershwin), 9, 11,
    94
    Houston Grand Opera
        production, 11
    telecast, 132
Porpora, Nicola, 156
Price, Janet, 126
Price, Leontyne, 132, 149
Prime donne, 4, 62–63, 143
Prince Igor (Borodin), 79
    "Polovtsian Dances," 79
Prompter's box, 140
Puccinni, Giacomo, 7, 8, 13, 14,
    19, 22, 28, 67, 75, 78, 128
    Girl of the Golden West by, 149
    La Bohème by. *See La Bohème*
    Madama Butterfly by, 8, 14, 23,
        58, 108
    Manon Lescaut by, 58
    Tosca by, 8, 14, 23, 58, 92, 136
    Turandot by, 19, 23, 92
Purcell, Henry, 4
    Dido and Aeneas by, 81–82
Putnam, Ashley, 96, 124

Queler, Eve, 125

Radames (tenor role in *Aida*), 35,
    36, 37, 38, 55
Radio City Music Hall, 91
Radio France, 126
Rake's Progress, The (Stravinsky),
    20
Rameau, Jean-Philippe, 109, 110,
    127
    Les Indes Galantes by, 78, 82
    Le Temple de la Gloire by, 78,
        82
    opera recordings, 125
Ramfis (basso role in *Aida*), 35, 37
Rapid divisions, 64, 65

RCA record company, 125
Realistic opera, 7
Recitativo (recitative), 5, 6
  accompagnato, 5, 45
  secco, 5, 45
Recording companies, 125
Regional opera, 95–100
Reiner, Fritz, 150
Reinhardt, Max
  Everyman, Salzburg Festival
    production, 117
Renaissance Florence, 1–2, 9
Rethberg, Elisabeth, 35
Ricci brothers
  Crispino e la Comare by, 126
Rigoletto (Verdi), 6, 14, 58, 92,
    113
  at opening of Suez Canal, 35
  "Caro nome" (soprano aria), 14
  quartet from, 6
Rimsky-Korsakov, Nikolai
  Le Coq d'Or by, 149
Rinaldo (Handel)
  Houston Grand Opera
    production, 124
Ring operas (Wagner), 58, 66,
    103, 116
  Seattle Opera/Pacific Northwest
    festival production, 102
Robbins, Jerome, 79
Robert le Diable (Meyerbeer),
  "Ballet of the Ghostly Nuns,"
    79
Rodgers, Richard, and Oscar
  Hammerstein II, 9
Rodolfo (tenor role in La
  Bohème), 24–28 passim, 55,
    136, 137
Romantic age, 156
Roméo et Juliette (Gounod), 8,
    16, 133
Rome Opera, 113
Rosina (soubrette in The Barber of
  Seville), 71, 141
Ross, Glynn, 103
Rossini, Gioacchino, 5, 19, 64,
    125, 146, 154, 156
  The Barber of Seville by, 19, 22,
    71, 127, 128, 141, 144
  bel canto operas, 66

Otello by, 128
overtures, 119
William Tell by, 19
Royal Ballet (Covent Garden
  London), 112
Rubini, Giovanni Battista, 154,
    156, 157

Sacred Music Society of New York,
    126
Salome (R. Strauss)
  "Dance of the Seven Veils," 81
Salzburg Festival (Salzburg,
  Austria), 116–17, 121
  Grosses Festspielhaus, 117
San Diego Opera, 96, 106
San Diego Opera Verdi Festival,
    96, 106
San Francisco Opera, 93, 106
  telecasts, 129
Santa Fe Opera Festival, 100–1,
    106, 123, 138
Sarti, Giuseppe, 50
Satire, 7
Savoy operas, 141
Scenery, 2
  Baroque, 3
Scènes de la Vie de Bohème
  (Murger), 23, 28
Schaunard (baritone role in La
  Bohème), 24, 27
Schipa, Tito, 157
Schoenberg, Arnold, 8
Schönbrunn Palace Theater, 114
Schwann catalogue, 125
Schreier, Peter, 157
Scotti, Antonio, 151, 153
Seattle Opera, 98, 103, 107
  Wagner's Ring production, 102
Seidl, Anton, 72
Sembrich, Marcella, 88, 153
  Letter Duet with Emma Eames,
    141
Senesino (castrato), 155
Shakespeare, William
  Hamlet by, 43
Shaw, George Bernard, 3, 91
Shenandoah, 98
Show Boat (Kern), 9
Siddons, Sarah, 146

Siebel (mezzo-soprano role in
    Faust), 30, 31, 32, 133
Siegfried (Wagner), 18
Siepi, Cesare, 51
Sills, Beverly, 72, 89, 91, 92, 149
Singer, 2, 61–63
    fat, 145
    vocal criteria, 63–68
Singing
    French style, 8, 15–16, 30
Singing actor, 68–72
Singspiel (song-play), 5, 6
Solos, 2
Solti, Georg, 74
Sondheim, Stephen
    Sweeney Todd by, 9, 11, 155
Song-play (Singspiel), 5, 6
Sontag, Henriette, 146, 154
Soprano voice, 4
    castrati, 134–35
    spinto, 38
    women, 133–34
Soubrette, 71
Souez, Ira, 118
Sound of Music, The (Rodgers
    and Hammerstein), 9
South America, opera in, 114
South Pacific (Rodgers and
    Hammerstein), 9, 155
Speech-song (Sprechgesang), 9
Spinto voice range, 38
Spohr, Louis, 128
Spoleto Festival, Italy, 101, 120
Spoleto Festival, U.S.A., 101, 107
Spontini, Gasparo, 110
    La Vestale by, 127
    recordings, 125
Sprechgesang (speech-song), 9
Stage director, 75–76
Star system, 62
Stories, 2, 5, 6, 8
Strauss, Johann II
    Die Fledermaus by, 6, 7, 141
Strauss family, 6
Strauss, Richard, 7
    Arabella by, 124
    Ariadne auf Naxos by, 149
    Capriccio by, 92–93
    Der Rosenkavalier by, 18, 77,
        149

Die Frau ohne Schatten by, 77,
        78
    Elektra by, 149
    Le Bourgeois Gentilhomme by,
        82
    Salome by, 81
Stravinsky, Igor
    The Rake's Progress by, 20
Style, 64–65
    French, 66–67
Suez Canal, 35
Sullivan, Arthur, 7, 141
Supervia, Conchita, 156
Sutherland, Joan, 65, 68, 156, 157
"Swanee," 141
Sweden
    ballet in, 82
    opera in, 3
    See also Drottningholm Festival
Sweeney Todd (Sondheim), 9, 11,
    155
Sydney (Australia) Opera House,
    114, 115
Szell, Georg, 150

Taglioni, Marie, 79
Tamagno, Francesco, 114, 153
Tamburini, Antonio, 154, 156
Tannhäuser (Wagner), 6, 18,
    39–43
    ballet, 40, 56, 79
    coloratura, 66
    "Dich, teure Halle," 41
    "Elisabeth's Intercession," 42
    first or Dresden version, 40
    "Forgiveness," 42
    "Hymn to Venus," 40, 42, 43
    love arias, 55
    love duet, 55
    Metropolitan Opera production,
        41, 116
    "O du mein holder Abendstern,"
        55
    "O evening star," 42, 43
    orchestra, 57
    overture, 40
    "Parisian Bacchanale," 40
    "Pilgrim's Chorus," 40, 42
    "Repentance," 42

second or Paris version, 40
story, 39–43
"Tannhäuser's Agony," 42
Venusberg ballet, 79
"Venusberg Theme," 40, 42
vocal techniques, 57, 58
Tannhäuser (tenor role in
    Tannhäuser), 39–40
Teatro alla Scala, 108–9, 120. See
    also La Scala
Teatro Amazones (Manaus,
    Brazil), 114
Teatro Colón (Buenos Aires,
    Argentina), 114
Teatro la Fenice (Venice, Italy),
    113
Teatro Regio (Turin, Italy), 23
Teatro San Carlo (Naples, Italy),
    113
Technique, 63
Telemann, Georg Philipp, 4, 155
    opera recordings, 125
Television, 68, 69
    opera on, 129–32
Tenors, 4, 65–66
    buffo roles, 71–72
    chest tones, 65
    head tones, 65–66
Texas Opera Theater, 94
Théâtre de la Monnaie (Brussels),
    113
Théâtre National de L'Opéra
    (Paris Opéra), 120. See also
    Paris Opéra
Theme (leitmotiv), 39
Thomas, Ambroise
    Hamlet by, 96
Tibbett, Lawrence, 140, 149
Tonal music, 8
Tone, 63
Torquato Tasso (Donizetti), 126
Tosca (Puccini), 8, 14, 23, 58, 91,
    92, 137
    "Vissi d'arte," 136
Toscanini, Arturo, 23, 35, 53,
    72–73, 74, 83, 88, 103, 117,
    137, 140, 149–51
Tragédies-lyriques, 78
Traubel, Helen, 137, 147
Treemonisha (Joplin), 94, 95

Trills, 57, 58, 64
Tristan und Isolde (Wagner), 137
Turandot (Puccini), 19, 23, 92,
    149

Una Cosa Rara (Martín y Soler),
    128
Unit sets, 77–78

Valentin (baritone role in Faust),
    30, 31, 33, 140
Valletti, Cesare, 157
Venus (mezzo-soprano role in
    Tannhäuser), 40
Verdi, Giuseppe, 6, 8, 14, 19, 58,
    80, 96, 127
    Aida by. See Aida
    ballet, 79
    complete opera recordings, 125
    Falstaff by, 35, 97, 137, 144
    I Lombardi by, 58, 103
    Il Trovatore by, 14–15, 58, 103,
        144
    La Traviata by, 14, 58, 103, 144
    Luisa Miller by, 90–91
    Nabucco by, 58
    Otello by, 6, 16, 35, 66, 108,
        128
    overture, 56
    Requiem by, 103
    Rigoletto by, 6, 14, 58, 92, 113
    San Diego Opera Verdi Festival,
        103
Verdy, Violette, 80
Verismo opera, 7, 22, 23, 24, 25,
    67, 156
Verona Festival (Verona, Italy),
    84, 119, 122
Videotape, 68
Vienna
    operetta, 6–7, 9
Vienna Philharmonic. See Vienna
    State Opera Orchestra
Vienna State Opera, 89, 107,
    110–11, 121
    broadcasts, 129
Vienna State Opera Orchestra,
    110–11
Vienna Volksoper (Folk Opera),
    114, 138

Villa-Lobos, Heitor, 100
Vivaldi, Antonio, 4, 136, 155
  Orlando Furioso by, 98
Vocal criteria, 63–68
  diction, 63
  embellishment, 63, 65
  rapid divisions, 64, 65
  style, 64–65
  technique, 63
  tone, 63
Vocal techniques, 56–57, 58
Von Karajan, Herbert, 74, 141

Wagner (role in Faust), 31
Wagner, Richard, 7, 18, 22, 58,
    66, 75, 78, 79, 83, 98, 125,
    126–27
  Bayreuth Festival, 66, 103,
    115–16, 121
  Das Rheingold by, 18
  Die Meistersinger by, 39
  Die Walküre by, 18
  Der Fliegende Holländer by, 76
  leitmotiv (theme), 39
  Lohengrin by, 6, 39, 127
  music dramas, 39
  overture, 56
  Pacific Northwest Wagner
    Festival, 102, 103
  Parsifal by, 116
  Ring operas, 58, 66, 102, 103,
    116
  Siegfried by, 18

Tannhäuser by. See Tannhäuser
Tristan und Isolde by, 137
Wagner, Wieland, 116
Wagner, Wolfgang, 116
Wagnerian opera, 22
Walter, Bruno, 73, 74, 117, 150
Washington, D.C., Metropolitan
    Opera national tour, 100, 105
Weber, Carl Maria von, 146
  Der Freischütz by, 58
Weill, Kurt, 94
  Mahagonny by, 11
West Side Story, 79
Whoopee!, 98
William Tell (Rossini), 19
Wolf-Ferrari, Ermanno, 8
  Il Campiello by, 5, 128
  Il Segreto di Susanna by, 5
  recordings, 125
Wolfram (baritone role in
    Tannhäuser), 41
Wolf Trap, 100
Women
  singing roles as men, 133–34,
    136
Wozzeck (Berg), 8, 19

Yeoman of the Guard, The
    (Gilbert and Sullivan), 7

Zeffrelli, Franco, 77
Zerlina (lyric soprano role in Don
    Giovanni), 46–51 passim, 55